"So much of what can be most beautiful about our churches is summed up in that single (and often overlooked) word: honour. Adam Ramsey's book offers compelling insights that will help us all to make our church communities better reflect the love and glory of Jesus. This is vital to the health of our churches, and a vital key to having an impact on the world around us."

SAM ALLBERRY, Associate Pastor, Immanuel Nashville;
Co-Author, *You're Not Crazy: Gospel Sanity for Weary Churches*

"Surely one of the most neglected commands in the Western church is the command to outdo one another in showing honour (Romans 12:10). In a culture obsessed with self-love, self-promotion and self-fulfilment, the call to value others above ourselves can sound unreasonably hard and possibly harmful. Adam Ramsey helps us understand why honour among members and leaders is essential for the health of our churches, and how it can be a beautiful witness in our communities. He offers a compelling vision of a prayerful people committed to humble love, thoughtful encouragement and Christ-exalting service. This is a people I want to be part of! I pray this book will be widely read and that the church of Christ will shine more brightly as a result."

CAROLYN LACEY, Author, *Say the Right Thing*
and *(Extra)Ordinary Hospitality*

"I am thrilled to recommend Adam Ramsey's excellent new book. Having worked alongside Adam for close to a decade, I can attest to his exceptional character and unwavering commitment to living out what he writes in this book. In each chapter, Adam explores the true essence of honor within the church, showing us how we rightly honor God and one another through humility, biblical competitiveness and godly leadership. His insights are not just words on pages but a reflection of the honorable man he is. I wholeheartedly recommend Honor as an instructive, convicting and inspiring read that mirrors the wisdom and integrity of its author."

BRIAN HOWARD, President, Acts 29

"In this work, my friend Adam Ramsey shows us that a culture of honor is God's design for God's people. Our churches need this— not only a biblical theology of honor but a biblical experience of it. Creating a culture of honor is a vital way we can carry out Jesus' command to love one another, and in doing so, communicate to a watching world how the gospel truly changes lives and relationships, to the honor and praise of God."

TONY MERIDA, Pastor, Imago Dei Church, Raleigh, NC; Author, *Love Your Church* and *Gather*

"Honor: what an incredibly misused or ignored word. Depending on your church background, it can evoke a myriad of feelings. And yet, it is not a word we can pretend simply does not exist. We are exhorted by the Scriptures to "outdo one another in showing honour". Paul's words beg the question, "how?" And in this wonderfully thoughtful book, my friend Adam guides us toward the answers. With wit and grace, he points us to a better way of being God's people. What a beautiful invitation!"

LÉONCE B. CRUMP JR, *Founding Pastor, Renovation Church, Atlanta*

"As someone who has been under Adam's leadership for the past decade, I have witnessed him to be both honouring, and honourable, in the way he loves and serves those around him. What is written in these pages has been lived before it was penned. The book you are holding paints a picture of the relational beauty of God's kingdom being revealed in the lives of his people. And when his people rightly bestow honour upon one another, we get a glimpse of what the world is meant to be (and one day will be). I urge you to take these words in, and, by the Spirit's power, to live them out. Your church will be a truer and more beautiful reflection of the kingdom of Jesus because of it."

LAURA HAAS, Director of Ministries & Women's Director at Liberti Church, Gold Coast, Australia

honour

ADAM RAMSEY

Honour

Loving Your Church by Building One Another Up

© 2024 Adam Ramsey

Published by:
The Good Book Company

thegoodbook.com | thegoodbook.co.uk
thegoodbook.com.au | thegoodbook.co.nz | thegoodbook.co.in

Original series cover design by Faceout Studio | Art direction and design by André Parker

ISBN: UK/Aus/ROW 9781784989705 | US 9781784989668
JOB-007659 | Printed in India

CONTENTS

FOREWORD

BY ALISTAIR BEGG

Just as our homes have a "feel" to them, so do our church gatherings. The Dutch have a word that is almost untranslatable: *gezellig*. It describes a place—a gathering, that is attractive, sociable, friendly, welcoming, comfortable, even cozy.

Our churches should be marked by much more than that, but never less. And a key to being that kind of church is to be one that is marked by an honoring of one another.

I have benefitted greatly from this book, especially as its publication comes at a time when the very notion of the biblical emphasis on the priority and necessity of a gathered community is being challenged. It is becoming increasingly fashionable, even desirable, to construct a digital alternative that makes it possible for us to design and control our environment. If physical friendships can be replaced by smartphones and online chat during the week, then why not extend that to church life? After all, as the pastor and author Christopher Ash has observed, the local church is not made up of people with whom we would naturally choose to spend our holidays!

At no other time in history has it been possible to be "together" while we are actually apart. Creating an online network is vastly different from the togetherness that the Bible describes and demands. We are not called to grow up in digital networks but in communities that honor God and each other, and that begins by being present.

The temptation to isolation is not a 21st-century phenomenon. The writer of Hebrews exhorted his readers to make sure that they did not hold themselves aloof from the church gatherings as some had begun to do—because it is in that context that we learn how to stir up one another to love and good works (Hebrews 10:24-25). We are not members of a club, held together by shared interests—we are members of the body of Christ, shaped by grace.

In the early 1970s, my wife and I spent some time with the members of a church plant in a housing scheme in Edinburgh. The average age of the congregation was very young and most were new believers. Some had, in their previous life, been members of opposing gangs. Honor in that realm had much to do with being tough—but now they had become tender. It was profoundly moving to be present as former enemies honored one another biblically, singing to each other the song "I Love You with the Love of the Lord", with its glorious line, "I can see in you the glory of my King".

I am similarly moved today when I look out on our congregation and see the way in which the lives of people who would ordinarily never be in the company of one another are being wonderfully woven together in a tapestry of grace, building one another up and spurring one another on.

In commending this book to you, I freely acknowledge the challenge it brings to me first, both as a Christian and as a pastor. To be a church permeated by biblical honor requires church leaders to be honorable people—we cannot demand an honor that we do not deserve. Since a church does not progress beyond the spiritual progress of its leaders, Adam Ramsey's book calls those of us in leadership to examine ourselves. As the 17th-century pastor Richard Baxter reminded ministers in his day, "The honor of your Lord and master, and of his holy truth, doth lie more on you than other men ... It follows that we should not expect [a church] to be living honorable lives towards outsiders and one another when the leadership has failed to live in light of the word of the prophet."

But the call to be honorable and to honor others is not reserved for pastors. Scripture also requires church members to be ready to honor others—for us all to look more quickly to the interests and encouragement of those in our church than ourselves, and to be ready to humbly submit to those the Lord has called to shepherd the local flock we are part of.

In this book, Adam Ramsey shows us not only why we are to honor one another but what it looks like in the life of the local church. In this sense, you have in your hands an invitation—an invitation to cause your church to become more and more *gezellig*. I trust that you will find it clarifying, stimulating, encouraging and challenging, just as I have.

Alistair Begg
Bible Teacher, Truth For Life

INTRODUCTION: REDEEMING A MISUSED WORD

I know, I know. Some of you (my American friends) are already slightly concerned that I don't even know how to spell the word, given that I've opted to use my native Australian-English spelling of honour throughout the pages that follow. Others of you, wherever you live in the world and however you spell the word, are perhaps a little nervous picking up a book with this title.

And I honestly don't blame you.

For some of us, this word *honour* comes with quite a bit of baggage. Perhaps you have experienced the toxicity of a church culture where this word was twisted for the personal gain of those in leadership roles—where, like a velvet fist, "honour" was used as cover for unquestioning submission, spiritual manipulation, or even outright abuse. Or perhaps you have experienced a different kind of brokenness, where there is an absence of honour in the church. Neither of these are what the church is meant to look like, and my hope in this opening chapter is to tread a biblical pathway that avoids both of these ditches.

But before I do, let me paint you a picture of our destination. What if it were possible to redeem this word—*honour*—and reinfuse it with the fullness of biblical beauty that God intends? What *is* the togetherness of your church meant to look like? What *could* a culture of true honour look like?

Imagine a church where each and every person was serious about Jesus' command to sacrificially love one another *in the same way* that they have been loved by him; a church that honoured both his example and his commands in their esteem for each other. A Christian community where the only competitiveness was in the sincere desire to outdo each other in building one another up. A church where gratitude and gospel-motivated service to Jesus was the most normal thing in the world, and it spilled over horizontally into relationships with others in the church and into the surrounding community. Where repentance of sin was regular and real; where forgiveness was readily extended; where holiness was pursued and faithfulness was praised. A place where a heartfelt eulogy of the good in each other wasn't withheld until a person lay in a coffin, but was offered up freely, sincerely and regularly.

Imagine a church where men and women refused to make assumptions about each other's motives when they disagreed, instead giving one another the benefit of the doubt in a spirit of humility; where patience was esteemed more highly than politics; where leaders dignified God's people by refusing to use them and instead consistently cared for them, and where members gladly gave themselves to following such leaders in a spirit of unity, trust, and willing cooperation, out of reverence for Christ. A church where honour was not just unidirectional (from members to leaders) but omnidirectional (from *all*, to *all*), because nothing was more important to everyone than glorifying God by following Jesus into a life of humility—a way of living that Tim Keller called "the freedom of self-forgetfulness".[1]

Deep down, every one of us longs for this. And we need not wait for heaven to experience it. A right understanding of honour is vital to healthy churches. Its presence or absence is a barometer for humility—and God has made clear again and again that any community of professing Christians that is not marked by humility is opposed by him. For "God opposes the proud but gives grace to the humble" (James 4:6).

When honour is perverted into something that is self-serving or when it is absent altogether, it indicates that our gaze is still far too much upon ourselves. Yet when we are so impressed with Jesus that we are free from needing to be impressive ourselves, a biblical culture of

---

1 Timothy Keller, *The Freedom of Self-Forgetfulness* (10Publishing, 2012).

honour will permeate our churches. That is a foretaste of the world to come. And that's what every one of us is really aching to know.

When practiced with purity and sincerity, honour is glorious. But that still begs the question: what exactly is it and to whom should it be given?

WHAT IS HONOUR?

Honour is both a word and concept that is mentioned hundreds of times throughout the Bible. At its most fundamental level, it means to value rightly and treat with appropriate reverence and respect. Particularly when it comes to those with authority. In the Scriptures, we are called to honour God above all else (Revelation 4:11). We are to honour our fathers and mothers in our homes (Exodus 20:12), elders and leaders in our churches (1 Timothy 5:17), masters or employers in our places of work (Ephesians 6:5), and governors and civil leaders with authority in our societies (1 Peter 2:17). Yet honour is not merely something that is directed upward, but also *outward*. Husbands are commanded to show honour to their wives (1 Peter 3:7), widows are to be honoured within the church (1 Timothy 5:3), and in case we missed anyone, 1 Peter 2:17 commands, "Honour everyone". When used as a verb, it means to "magnify" or "give weight to".

Honour, then, is a posture of life that exalts and rejoices over both God and others. It is a lens of looking at God and honouring his glory, and then recognising that glory being woven into each person (on account of us being made in God's image—the *imago Dei*), or being woven into a position of authority. Romans 13:1 reminds us that there is something of God's glory that is revealed in earthly positions of authority. As we will see, honour is about giving appropriate weight to *both*, thus glorifying God and respecting one another. In light of the breadth and repetition of it in our Bibles, clearly this is not something we should brush over or take lightly.

While there is much we could say about honour in the home, the workforce or the world, the focus of this book will be about honour in the church. What is honour meant to look like among *Christians*? What is honour meant to look like towards Christian *leaders*? What kind of Christian leaders *are* we to honour, and what kind should we *refuse* to honour?

We've briefly named what honour is, and we will explore it further over the coming pages. But if we are going to recover any meaningful ground towards experiencing honour's true power in our churches, we also need to name upfront what honour is *not* and *must never be*. Strongly and unequivocally. As I've already mentioned, there are two ditches we can fall into on this subject. The first is where honour becomes manipulative. The second is where honour is missing altogether.

DITCH #1: WHERE "HONOUR" IS MANIPULATIVE

Sadly, honour can be distorted into something that is spiritually manipulative. And when it is, it inevitably and tragically sabotages a right experience with God and others in the local church. While this can play out in many forms, it usually boils down to two fundamental misunderstandings of honour.

The first is a version of prosperity theology—a widespread unbiblical and heretical teaching—that turns God into a cosmic genie who will shower his people with blessing, riches, health and long life if they will only rub the lamp in the right way, with enough faith. In this system, which bears an uncanny resemblance to a spiritual multi-level marketing scheme, the purpose of showing honour in the church is promoted as a get-rich-quick solution; a means to an end for upward mobility in the kingdom of God.

Yet despite what numerous books would have you believe, honour is *not* something we do in order to "position ourselves for blessing" or "attract God's favour". It is not a key through which we "unlock heaven" or a guarantee that will get God to give us our deepest desires. The way that some teachers speak about "honour" distorts God and diminishes honour into a Christianised version of the secular philosophy of the law of attraction. But biblical honour isn't self-seeking. Prosperity theology says, *Jesus, I'll honour you as a way to improve my life.*

Biblical theology says, *Jesus, I'll honour you because you are better than life*. To reduce honour to self-serving purposes is dishonourable in the highest degree; as are those who teach this.

The second way honour can be practiced perversely is when those with authority in a local church employ it in a way that elevates their own comfort and power, while using and dehumanising those under their authority. Or put more bluntly: *internships*. While there are certainly plenty of exceptions where churches do this very well, for the past few decades, many a ministry internship (at least in the West) has meant paying a lot of money to do a lot of free work for the church or for their church leader personally, in exchange for a poor theological education, a distorted experience of biblical leadership, and a lot of disappointment.

In the church that I pastor, there are literally dozens of men and women who were used by pastors and leaders in former churches: who, under the guise of "honouring them", were reduced to something similar to ecclesiastical slave-labour. I could tell countless stories of those who were instructed to clean their pastor's house each weekend, rise before the sun did to wash their jet-skis, put in 50-hour work weeks without pay, stand quietly behind them in the church foyer and hold their coffee (so they wouldn't be inconvenienced by having to hold their own drink), keep "undesirable people" away from approaching the pastor after the service, and serve those leaders without complaint or question... for Jesus.

Even if not being demanded to this kind of level—that is exploitation, not honour.

And nothing could be further from biblical Christianity, because nothing could be further from the example of Christ, who—having all authority—came not to be served, but to serve. He did not use his disciples to pad his own pockets or increase his comfort; he washed their feet. And in doing so, Jesus honoured them and showed them how those with authority are to use it. When teaching his followers who were in positions of power, Jesus could not have been more explicit with his profound message to invert the ways of the rest of the world:

> *You know that those who are regarded as rulers of the Gentiles lord it over them, and those in high positions act as tyrants over them. But it is not so among you. On the contrary, whoever wants to become great among you will be your servant, and whoever wants to be first among you will be a slave to all. For even the Son of Man did not come to be served, but to serve, and to give his life as a ransom for many.*
>
> *(Mark 10:42-45, CSB)*

Leadership in the church is to be marked by servanthood. As we will see in later chapters, we should gladly and willingly honour Christian leaders who are *honourable*.

But when they are not, when leaders act *dishonourably*, abusing their positions and those under their care, we are to honour God by calling them to repentance and removing them from a position of power, even as we refuse to dehumanise them.

DITCH #2: WHERE HONOUR IS MISSING

Sometimes, however, the problem is not that a church misuses honour but that it is missing honour altogether. Maybe some of us are afraid of practicing honour for fear of falling into the previous ditch we just looked at.

At this point, I need to be up front with you and lay my cards on the table. I am Australian. Mine is a culture to which honour does not come naturally. Established as a British prison colony just a couple of centuries ago, Australians to this day still carry somewhat of a prison mentality. We are quite often suspicious of authority and slightly infamous for the social phenomenon and phrase known as "tall poppy syndrome", where someone who is successful or gifted or has risen to a place of influence is cut down to size by those around them. The idea comes from the poppy—a flowering plant that tends to grow all at the same pace, to the same height. If one of the poppy flowers grows too high or too fast, the rest of the plant will strangle it at the root and bring it back down to earth. And a culture soaked in tall poppy syndrome is a great seedbed for a failure to honour one another in a biblical way.

Perhaps you have experienced a church culture that is absent of honour.

At its worst, this kind of culture is actively hostile: a place of tribalism and distrust, where words are weaponised and suspicion reigns. Leaders are suspicious of any who disagree with them; church members are suspicious of any in a position of authority or power; and the only person nobody would suspect of erring is themselves. Many a church split or relational rift can be traced to such an environment, where people in the midst of a conflict chose to believe the inerrancy of their own view while assuming the worst about any who questioned it.

At its best, church members in this kind of environment experience a pleasant aloofness; they are relative strangers who gather in the same building. People may be courteous and get along ok, but there is nothing relationally beautiful to write home about. An environment that is absent of honour reduces the vibrancy and colour of our life together in Christ to a dull and predictable relational greyness. And like the poppy plant, churches that lose sight of a biblical understanding of honour can become environments that pre-emptively strangle affirmation and encouragement, just in case anyone might be tempted to become proud or think they are more important than they are.

While it's true that Scripture does indeed teach that in light of God's grace, each member of Christ's body should be careful "not to think of himself more highly than he ought to think, but to think with sober judgement" (Romans 12:3), that is a command we are not to apply to *one another*, but to *ourselves*. Humility is vital, as we will see in a later chapter. But nowhere does Scripture call us to "humble one another". We are called repeatedly, however, to humble ourselves (James 4:10; 1 Peter 5:6). In fact, the unambiguous instruction given to Christians sharing life together is mentioned in Romans 12:10—where, rather incredibly, the apostle Paul tells us to, "Love one another with brotherly affection. Outdo one another in showing honour."

That's what it's meant to feel like, sound like and look like when we gather together. And that is the way Jesus wants us to go.

REDEEMING AND RECOVERING BIBLICAL HONOUR

So, just like with other important biblical truths, honour can be misused or neglected entirely. For those who've experienced this, the temptation to jettison the word altogether is entirely understandable. But in the same way that we should not throw out the entire concept of teaching within our churches because there is such a thing as bad teaching, neither should we abandon the concept of honour within our churches just because dishonourable leaders or environments exist. Just as unorthodox teaching in the church ought to be brought back into alignment with God's word, so too must unorthodox culture. In fact, if our churches are lacking in either, we can lay no authentic claim to being a biblically faithful church. The 20th-century theologian Francis Schaeffer wrote:

> *One cannot explain the explosive dynamite,*
> *the dunamis, of the early church apart from the*
> *fact that they practiced two things simultaneously:*
> *orthodoxy of doctrine and orthodoxy of community in*
> *the midst of the visible church, a community which the*
> *world could see. By the grace of God, therefore, the*
> *church must be known simultaneously for its purity of*
> *doctrine and the reality of its community.*[2]

The right response to a malpractice of honour within our churches is not to abandon honour, but to redeem it by practicing it biblically. My hope in this little book is to salvage the splendour of this word by recovering a right view of God and remembering that all honour belongs, first and foremost, to him. For it is only when we possess a God-centred view of honour that we will be able to truly honour the image of God within one another—valuing one another without commodifying one another. When God is rightly revered, we will willingly revere one another. When God's authority is understood and respected, we will then gladly respect honourable leaders that he has given to his church, for their flourishing.

---

2 Francis Schaeffer, *The Church Before the Watching World* (InterVarsity Press, 1970), p 62.

It won't be easy. It will require humility and honesty and patience. Yet if we will humble ourselves before God and one another, and sacrificially resolve to show dignity to one another in light of the gospel, then our churches will be oxygenated with strength and vitality. And the church of our time will truly shine like a city on a hill; a beautiful beacon of the world yet to come.

What if we were to give ourselves to a biblical vision of honour? To cultivating what one writer of old called "an epidemic of nobleness", in which men and women "become better and greater from gazing at [such an] example; more ready to do and dare; more willing to lift their eyes out of the mire of selfishness and the dust of anxiety and toil ... and by such sacrifices, become magnetic"?[3]

Honour. Let's redeem this biblical word. But more than that, let's refuse to settle for anything less than its biblical reality in our churches.

---

3 F.W. Farrar, *Saintly Workers* (Macmillan and Co, 1878), p 21, 24.

1. A CHURCH THAT HONOURS GOD ABOVE ALL

Wow... I thought to myself. *So this is what this moment feels like...*

Down on one knee, I shivered a little. It was winter, so some of that may have been the cold. But more likely it was the emotional flutter of a thousand butterflies that had been let loose in my stomach, working together to shake each quivering word out of my mouth, as if it were the first time I'd ever spoken them in English.

I was proposing.

But between the bruised leg (from being clipped by a car in a minor hit-and-run accident while I crossed the road after dinner) and the bruised ego (from failing to anticipate the high tide that had washed off the "Will you marry me?" message I had written in chalk on the rocks overlooking the Sydney harbour earlier that day), things weren't quite going to plan. And so I now played my final card.

There on one knee before Kristina, I nervously expressed my love for her, told her that there was no one in all the world like her, and that I wanted to spend my life with her. Then I repeated everything I had just said to her a second time. Not because she hadn't heard me, but because I couldn't quite coax *The Question* out of my mouth. Only after completing a third lap of this same verbal roundabout was I finally able to find the off-ramp and out came the question: *"Will you marry me?"*

Mercifully, she said yes.

Why does a man bend his knee when asking for a woman's hand in marriage? To honour her. To demonstrate his devotion to her in a posture that declares, "I am entirely yours. Your love has conquered me. I treasure you and honour you."

There are other occasions in our lives where we assume a posture like this, too—yet not out of loving devotion, but out of recognition for legitimate authority. Why do people kneel before a monarch, rise when a judge enters a courtroom, or raise their hands when commanded to by an officer of the law? Because to do so is to recognise and honour their authority. These are outward acts that signify submission and declare, *"I am not in charge here"*.

Why do many Christians kneel in prayer, or rise to their feet in church when the Scripture is read, or raise their hands in worship? Because to do so is a recognition of God's authority; actions that likewise declare, *"God, I am not in charge here. You are."* This is why John records that all of heaven, "fell on their faces before the throne and worshipped God, saying, 'Amen! Blessing and glory and wisdom and thanksgiving and honour and power and might be to our God for ever and ever! Amen'" (Revelation 7:11-12). Elsewhere, in Romans 13:1 Paul reminds Christians that God is not only the highest authority but the source of all human authority: "Let every person be subject to the governing authorities. For there is no authority except from God, and those that exist have been instituted by God." Christians are to honour those in power over them with willing submission and to resist or disobey only when those authorities demand us to go against God's authority.

In fact, something we will see again and again throughout this book is that all the honour we give to other humans is merely an extension of honouring God himself. We respect governing authorities because they bear instituted authority from God, and we esteem one another because each person you meet bears the image of God. As Peter summarises in four succinct statements, specifically directed to those who claim to be servants of Jesus: "Honour everyone. Love the brothers and sisters. Fear God. Honour the emperor" (1 Peter 2:17 CSB).

Honouring God includes both of these realities: "I am entirely yours" and "You are entirely in charge". It comprises both love-compelled devotion and authority-recognising reverence. Perhaps you can remember times in your own life where a sense of God's glory and greatness and majesty were intensified in your experience, convincing you of the sheer *Godness* of God at the deepest level of your being—times where you found yourself overwhelmed in worship or in prayer, and the only appropriate response was to fall to your knees and acknowledge that he is worthy of all your devotion, of all that you *are*.

All true honour is based in a faithful response to the greatness of God's authority and the goodness of God's love. And since God is unequalled in both, he alone is worthy of being honoured in the most exclusive and exalted way we can: *through worship*. Barely a few paragraphs into his first letter to Timothy, Paul prays in this way, declaring, "To the King of ages, immortal, invisible, the only God, *be honour and glory* for ever and ever. Amen" (1 Timothy 1:17, emphasis added).

So how do we honour God in the way that he desires? Biblical honour towards God is a three-legged stool that includes how we think about him (sound doctrine), how we live before him (faithful obedience), and the motive that produces each of these (genuine love).

HONOUR GOD THROUGH SOUND DOCTRINE

On the opening page of his classic, *The Knowledge of the Holy*, A.W. Tozer famously wrote that, "What comes into our minds when we think about God is the most important thing about us".[4] God is honoured when his people think thoughts about him and teach truth about him that is consistent with how he has revealed his character and nature to us—otherwise known as sound doctrine.

And, in case words like "doctrine" or "theology" make your eyes glaze over a little, just remember this: doctrine is a set of beliefs about God. Theology is simply what we think about God, or "the study of God". Both matter deeply, because what we believe and think about God deeply matters. When someone asked Jesus about the most important commandment of all, the response that he gave included loving God with all our *mind*, as well as all our heart, soul and strength (Mark 12:28-30).

After encouraging Timothy to faithfully pass on what he has taught to him, the apostle Paul declares, "If anyone teaches false doctrine and does not agree with the sound teaching of our Lord Jesus Christ and with the teaching that promotes godliness, he is conceited and understands nothing" (1 Timothy 6:3-4 CSB). The elders of a church are to "give instruction in sound doctrine and also to rebuke those who contradict it" (Titus 1:9), and are commanded: "But as for you, teach what accords with sound doctrine (Titus 2:1). We'll focus on this area later in the book when we explore what the Bible says honourable leadership within the church is to look like,

---

4 Aiden Wilson Tozer, *The Knowledge of the Holy* (Authentic Media, 2016), p 1.

but for now we need simply to see that God is honoured when we think and speak the truth about him.

Conversely, God is *not* honoured when we think or teach things about him that are not true—when he is painted as other than what he is. Consider it at a personal level: do you feel honoured when you hear of someone saying things about you that aren't true? Of course not. At best you feel misrepresented. At worst, you feel slandered. Dishonoured. That's what false teaching is: a misrepresentation and slander of God. And that gets to the root of humanity's fundamental problem: a failure to rightly honour God by exchanging the truth about God for a lie. In Romans 1:21-25, Paul writes:

> *For although they knew God, they did not honour him as God or give thanks to him, but they became futile in their thinking, and their foolish hearts were darkened. Claiming to be wise, they became fools, and exchanged the glory of the immortal God for images resembling mortal man and birds and animals and creeping things. Therefore God gave them up in the lusts of their hearts to impurity, to the dishonouring of their bodies among themselves, because they exchanged the truth about God for a lie and worshipped and served the creature rather than the Creator, who is blessed for ever! Amen.*

Our churches honour God when, with open Bibles, we refuse to believe what is *not* true about God and hold fast to the sound doctrine of what *is* true about him. In the same way that a blurry or discoloured photo of my wife fails to accurately represent her beauty, so too does false teaching fail to accurately portray the beauty of God. Good theology is like a high-resolution photo that reveals God's likeness. In this way, sound doctrine honours God because it reflects who he is. But there is another reason why holding to sound doctrine in your life brings honour to God: what you believe shapes how you live. That is as true for an individual Christian as it is for a local church.

HONOUR GOD THROUGH FAITHFUL OBEDIENCE

While true honour of God must begin with a right view of who he is and what he has said, it cannot end there. True honour includes what we *do*. Imagine I went to one of my children and said, "Come outside, we're going to work together in the yard today." And they respond, "Ok, Dad!"

But an hour goes by, and they are nowhere to be seen.

It's a beautiful day outside and so I call their name and say again, "Come outside! We're working together in the yard today!" From within the house, I hear a muffled yell back, "Ok, Dad! I will!"

Yet several more hours go by, and still there is no sign of them.

As the sun begins to set, I finally go inside, and upon finding them ask, "Where have you been? Did you hear what I said to you?" And they say, "Dad, I totally heard you. Your words meant so much to me that I spent time meditating over them. I committed those words to memory so that I'd never forget your instruction. I even studied what you said and used the *Logos* software on your computer to break down each word so I could really discover the fullness of their meanings. In fact, your words were so impactful to me, I spent the afternoon telling every kid on the street to work with their own fathers in the yard today!"

The example is a little far-fetched, but you get the idea. Our actions give weight to the sincerity of our professed beliefs. In the same way that a husband does not honour his wife by lavishing her with compliments while sleeping with another woman and an employee does not honour his CEO by thanking her for his position while embezzling company funds, nor do Christians honour God if we sing of his glory while living for our own. Where hypocrisy is present and unrepented of in our lives, authentic honour of God is missing. Which is why Jesus asked his disciples, "Why do you call me 'Lord, Lord,' and don't do the things I say?" (Luke 6:46 CSB). God is exalted in the lives of his people when they give themselves to both sound doctrine *and* faithful, Spirit-powered obedience.

But there is one more piece that is so vital to a right honouring of God that the Lord rebuked its absence among his people in both the Old and New Testaments...

HONOUR GOD THROUGH GENUINE LOVE

In Matthew 15:7-9, Jesus quoted Isaiah and called out the disconnect of sound doctrine and deep devotion when they have the wrong motive:

You hypocrites! Well did Isaiah prophesy of you, when he said:

"This people honours me with their lips, but their heart is far from me; in vain do they worship me, teaching as doctrines the commandments of men."

According to Jesus, the fundamental hypocrisy of many who claim to know him is not to do with what they say about him or to do with how they act, but about their communion with him. They lack authenticity in relationship with God. They love their theology more than the God whom that theology reveals. They live Christian lives—as far as those around them can tell—but their hearts are absent of genuine love. Elsewhere, Jesus said of the religious leaders of his time, "They do all their deeds to be seen by others. For they make their phylacteries broad and their fringes long, and they love the place of honour at feasts and the best seats in the synagogues and greetings in the marketplaces and being called rabbi by others" (Matthew 23:5-7).

Think of it like this. Imagine I buy my wife a stunning bouquet of her favourite kind of flowers on our anniversary: Australian natives. As I hand them to her, I courteously inform her: "It's our anniversary. Here are some flowers." Then as her face lights up with gratitude and she begins to say thank you, imagine I interrupt her and say, "Don't mention it. It seemed like the right thing to do, particularly in light of all the things I want you to do for me over this coming week." Would she feel honoured by my actions? Not if they come from a place of transactional, loveless duty, rather than authentic, relational affection. God is not honoured by true words about him that come from a heart that is far from him. He wants the substance of who we are—our very hearts. Anything less does not honour him in truth. Our motives matter.

A wise practice that every one of us can give ourselves to from time to time is pausing to examine our hearts with the question, "*Why* am I doing what I do for God?" Is it because I love him? Or has my heart drifted and found other reasons for the rhythms of my discipleship to Christ? Why do I attend church, gather with my small group, sing songs of worship, give of my finances, and use my gifts to build up those around me in my church?

Is my activity for Jesus still coming from a place of love for Jesus?

It is of no small importance that when the risen Jesus was restoring Peter in John 21 (Peter who had three times publicly denied his friend and Saviour, just as Jesus had prophesied he would), Jesus linked Peter's *work* for him with his *love* for him. Three times, he asked Peter, "Do you love me?" (v 15-17). Three times, he followed up his question to Peter with a commission to feed, shepherd, and watch over his sheep—God's people. Jesus already knew Peter's answer to his question. He wasn't asking for his own sake but for Peter's, and for ours. Where in your life might you need to make some space to be alone with God, re-examine your motives and bring them back into alignment to the gospel?

A CHURCH THAT HONOURS GOD TOGETHER

How do we honour God? By recognising his glory and authority with our heads, our hands and our hearts. On that three-legged stool of our doctrine, our actions, and our affections, all three legs are vital to magnifying God in both our individual lives and in the shared life of our church. A church honours God to the extent that God is the orbital centre that all of that church's worship, teaching, theology, community, and mission revolves around. While a healthy church most certainly will bless us and encourage us, it doesn't exist for us. Your church exists for *God*. Could there be any higher goal for us as followers of Jesus, than to honour him in all that we do, with all that we are?

It's true that none of us can ever honour God enough— not in this world or even the one to come. His love towards us—that we know in part now—is of a breadth and length and height and depth and quality "that surpasses knowledge" (Ephesians 3:19). But if his grace has opened your heart wide to him, then your deepest desire will be to honour him. To exalt him. To bow before him as you both recognise his authority yet revel in his love. To lift your voice in proclamation of him and in song to him. And to join your heart with the innumerable multitudes around the throne in Revelation 5:12, declaring with undiluted sincerity:

Worthy is the Lamb who was slain, to receive power and wealth and wisdom and might and honour and glory and blessing!

FOR REFLECTION

- Our honour of God includes both love-compelled devotion and authority-recognising reverence. Do you tend to emphasise one at the expense of the other? What happens when either one of these is missing?

- If someone asked you why sound doctrine matters when it comes to the way a church honours and loves God, how would you answer them?

- Consider the question we ended this chapter with: "Is my activity for Jesus still coming from a place of love for Jesus?" Reflect on that for a few minutes and, as the Spirit leads you, bring to God in repentance any areas of your life or ministry that need to be recalibrated to a motive of love.

2. A CHURCH THAT IS NOTORIOUS FOR HUMILITY

He was the most formidable man on earth, unrivalled in power and might. None could resist his will. All he desired, he possessed. But on this night, despite all his power, there was one adversary that successfully refused his will and stood beyond his reach: *sleep*. King Ahasuerus—ruler of the Persian Empire—ordered the book of memorable deeds to be brought to him and read aloud. Hoping to be lulled to sleep, instead, an event read out from the not-too-distant past piqued his attention: a man named Mordecai had saved his life from a pair of assassins. Upon learning that no reward had been given him, the king ordered in Haman—his most trusted advisor, who had just arrived at the palace—and asked him a question:

> *What should be done to the man whom the king delights to honour? (Esther 6:6)*

Being unaware of what had just unfolded and believing that he was the man the king was referring to, Haman began to list off a litany of his wildest dreams. *"Oh, your Majesty—you should dress such a man in your own royal robes, place a crown on his head and have him ride on your own royal horse, and then command the king's most noble officials to lead him through the city proclaiming, "Thus shall it be done to the man whom the king delights to honour!"* (v 8-9, paraphrased). The king looked pleased. Haman looked pleased. Scratch that—Haman likely looked like a child on Christmas morning, standing before a pile of presents, about to burst from happy anticipation. The one thing that Haman had given his life to was his reputation. He needed to be a somebody. He was the kind of man who was committed to honouring himself— putting himself first and putting himself forward, ever seeking the glory that comes from being a step higher than everyone else. And now he stood on the brink of having his deepest dream come true.

Go and do exactly as you have said, commanded the king.

For Mordecai.

Mordecai. Not only was Haman *not* going to be the one honoured by the king; he was required to publicly honour somebody he loathed. Mordecai was the one person who had refused to stroke Haman's super-sized ego. Mordecai was therefore the one person who Haman hated above all others—so much so that the entire reason Haman had come to the palace that evening was to ask the king's permission to hang Mordecai on a giant gallows he had constructed.

So it would be fair to assume that Haman was no longer happy. But since the king had commanded it, and since he was highly committed to not only self-exaltation but self-preservation, Haman obeyed. And as the story unfolds over the coming chapters of the book of Esther, all of Haman's self-serving treachery is brought into the light, and the king orders that he be executed. Haman found out that honouring himself did not lead to glory but to a gallows.

Before we can talk about the beauty of humility, we need to first consider the impact of its opposite; the great enemy of every person and every church—and the way that the devil became the devil: *self-honouring, self-seeking pride*.

THE NOOSE OF SELF-HONOUR

Honour beautifies the church, but it comes with a catch; a built-in kill-switch. When it is used wrongly—when honour is misdirected inward to ourselves rather than outward to God and others—that which is precious becomes poisonous. Why? Because self-honour is pride. And pride deforms us, warping the beauty of God's design and uglifying us with self-deception, just like it did to those once beautiful angels we now know as demons and devils. As Proverbs 16:18 warns us, "Pride goes before destruction, and a haughty spirit before a fall". And nowhere is this biblical principle demonstrated more obviously than in Haman. For, as the Bible repeatedly tells us, "God opposes the proud, but gives grace to the humble" (James 4:6; 1 Peter 5:5). Consider the small sampling of Scriptures below, each of which are worth reading slowly, so that we see just how opposed God is towards self-exaltation...

- You save a humble people, but your eyes are on the haughty to bring them down (2 Samuel 22:28).

- The Lord tears down the house of the proud (Proverbs 15:25).

- Before destruction a man's heart is haughty, but humility comes before honour (Proverbs 18:12).

- One's pride will bring him low, but he who is lowly in spirit will obtain honour (Proverbs 29:23).

- Behold I am against you, O proud one, declares the Lord GOD of hosts (Jeremiah 50:31).

- Everyone who exalts himself will be humbled, and he who humbles himself will be exalted (Luke 14:11).

When sought after for ourselves, honour is lethal. But when given away to others, honour becomes life-giving. Consider that last Scripture in Luke 14. Jesus was at the house of one of the leading Pharisees, and noticed how those who were invited were trying to position themselves in places of honour (v 1, 7). So he told them the following parable:

*When you are invited by someone to a wedding feast,
do not sit down in a place of honour, lest someone
more distinguished than you be invited by him, and he
who invited you both will come and say to you, "Give
your place to this person," and then you will begin
with shame to take the lowest place. But when you are
invited, go and sit in the lowest place, so that when your
host comes he may say to you, "Friend, move up higher."
Then you will be honoured in the presence of all who
sit at table with you. For everyone who exalts himself
will be humbled, and he who humbles himself will be
exalted. (Luke 14:8-11)*

The point Jesus is making is that life is found in the low
place. See yourself as the most important person in the
room and your misdirected honour will inevitably bring
you down. But when you take your eyes off yourself;
when your heart says with John the Baptiser "[Jesus]
must increase ... I must decrease" (John 3:30); when
like Paul you begin to see yourself as "the very least of
all the saints" (Ephesians 3:8); then you will come to a
remarkable, liberating realisation: *no one is beneath you.*
And when no one is beneath you, you are finally free.
"For you were called to freedom, brothers. Only do
not use your freedom as an opportunity for the flesh,
but through love serve one another" (Galatians 5:13).
Honour and humility go together.

THE FREEDOM OF HUMILITY

A similar lesson can be learned from the words of the Old Testament prophet, Isaiah. In Isaiah 57:15 we are reminded that the place of glory belongs to God alone: "I dwell in the high and holy place," says the Lord. When our pride draws us towards exalting ourselves, the kill-switch is activated and self-honour becomes self-destructive. But according to this same verse, there is another location that God inhabits; a place where his glory won't destroy us, but revives us: "I dwell in the high and holy place, *and also with him who is of a contrite and lowly spirit, to revive the spirit of the lowly, and to revive the heart of the contrite*" (emphasis added). In the place of humility, the low place, we meet with God and are renewed with life. So what's keeping us from making our home *there*? After all, the only thing we'll lose is a misdirected high view of ourselves that was going to ruin us anyway.

It should not surprise us that humility and honour are inseparable friends, always travelling together. The wisdom book of Proverbs reminds us that "One's pride will bring him low, but he who is lowly in spirit will obtain honour" (Proverbs 29:23). Again, "The fear of the LORD is instruction in wisdom, and *humility comes before honour*" (Proverbs 15:33, emphasis added). And that's exactly how the story of Haman and Mordecai ends: the one who sought honour for himself was humbled, and the one who sought humility was honoured. "The king took off his signet ring, which he had taken from Haman, and gave it to Mordecai. And Esther set Mordecai over the house of Haman" (Esther 8:2). Haman put himself in the high place and was brought low; Mordecai willingly went to the low place—not seeking honour for himself—and was exalted to the position that Haman once inhabited as the second most powerful man in the empire.

What might your church look like if every time you walked into the building, your first thought was not *"What am I going to get today?"*, but *"Isn't it amazing that I'm even a Christian? Isn't it utterly ridiculous that God has extended grace to someone like me?"* Only with the latter attitude, in the freedom of humility, will we ever begin to readily and sincerely honour one another. That's what humility looks like. It's not so much self-loathing but self-forgetfulness. Because humble people take God seriously (and not themselves), they're actually able to laugh at themselves. Because humble people aren't trying to impress one another, they're actually free to love one another. Instead of posturing to one another and draining the life out of one another, humble people have a renewing impact on each other's lives.

Is there a greater need in the church today?

In our culture of self-promotion, selfies and seeking validation through likes and followers, a church that is notorious for humility is a relational oasis—a place of renewal and life for those exhausted from pretending to be more than they actually are. Honour is at the very heart of our worship to God, and is woven into every act of love we experience from one another. In fact, honour is one of the acts that love *does*—as Paul reminds us, "[Love] does not boast, it is not proud. It does not dishonour others, it is not self-seeking" (1 Corinthians 13:4-5, NIV). Love at its truest and purest is a self-giving act of humility—being neither proud nor self-seeking. So when we are genuinely honouring another, we are no longer looking at ourselves, because the gospel has reoriented our eyes towards Jesus. And here's how we know we have begun to enter into such a reality: honest confession and repentance of sin gradually become normalised in our lives.

GOSPEL CULTURE: HONEST CONFESSION AND REPENTANCE

A couple of weeks ago, I was sitting in a room with a precious group of men and women who gather each week on a Tuesday night to open our Bibles and hearts to one another. We call these midweek small-groups in our church "gospel communities", because our goal together is not merely good fellowship or good advice, but to recalibrate our hearts to the good news. As Dietrich Bonhoeffer wrote, "the goal of all Christian community [is that we] meet one another as bringers of the message of salvation".[5] During our discussion that night, one of the men confessed the crippling shame he felt from a failure in his past and his lingering regret about it. It was a moment raw with vulnerability and honesty. It

---

5 Dietrich Bonhoeffer, *Life Together* (SCM Press Ltd, 1985), p 12.

was holy ground. Yet after he finished speaking, two things happened. First, his confession wasn't met with scolding but with the gospel. One by one, his brothers and sisters in Christ around the room pointed him to Jesus, reminding him that Jesus severed the power of shame when he took the shame of our every sin upon himself on the cross (Hebrews 12:2). Second, his honest confession broke through the pretence that we so often put on like a mask with one another, to hide our true selves. In the aftermath of his own confession, others around the room began to confess areas where they were struggling right now in the present. And we experienced together the reality that admission of weakness and honest confession aren't places to avoid but are our doorway into God's redemptive power.

Confessing our sins vertically brings *forgiving* impact, for as 1 John 1:9 reminds us, "If we confess our sins, he is faithful and just to forgive us our sins and to cleanse us from all unrighteousness." So by all means, let's do that first and frequently, confident that Jesus is the Saviour who is never fatigued in his willingness to forgive. My friend Ray Ortlund reminds us:

Do you really think, after the cross, your shame drives God away? Nope. Your shame is precisely where he can re-create you the most gloriously. You think you're disgusting to him? Wrong again. The worst things about you are where he loves you the most tenderly. God welcomes high-maintenance [people] who keep coming

back to him for more mercy and more mercy and more
*mercy, multiple times every day. He isn't **tired**, and he*
*isn't tired of **you**.*[6]

Yet confessing our sins horizontally, to one another, does something different. It brings *healing* impact. In James 5:16 we are told, "Confess your sins to one another and pray for one another, that you may be healed". Relationships within your church that are marked by vulnerability and truth and grace are the most important relationships you can cultivate in your walk as a follower of Jesus. These are relationships marked by humility, where telling the truth about our sin isn't weird and repenting of our sins against each other is normal. A gospel culture is one where shame is drowned in the waters of honest confession. It is a place where we honour one another, free from the need to pretend we are better than we are, because we are collectively convinced that Jesus is a better Saviour than any of us could dream of.

So don't seek honour. Seek Jesus. That's the only way our churches will become places notorious for humility, places of honour where honest confession and godly repentance are normalised. Imagine what our witness might be if the Christians of our time were to recover a reputation for being a humble people who aren't preoccupied with themselves or constantly promoting

---

6 Ray Ortlund, *The Death of Porn: Men of Integrity Building a World of Nobility* (Crossway, 2021), p 34.

themselves, because they are satisfied in the glory of Jesus. Imagine what would happen if we become a people who aren't afraid of confessing our sin when we get it wrong, because we are convinced that Jesus is the friend of sinners (Matthew 11:19) and that "if we confess our sins, he is faithful and just to forgive us our sins and to cleanse us from all unrighteousness" (1 John 1:9). Imagine what it would be like to be part of a people who have made peace with their weakness; who have exchanged a self-confident swagger for a holy limp; who have learned to say with Paul, "For the sake of Christ, then, I am content with weaknesses, insults, hardships, persecutions, and calamities. For when I am weak, then I am strong" (2 Corinthians 12:10). In other words, imagine what it would be like to be a people who gradually, but unmistakably, look more and more like Jesus.

Let's follow our Saviour into humility. Let's allow God to be the one who exalts us, rather than trying to climb over one another to places of importance. Let's find life in the low place. And as we do, let's hunt for ways to "love one another with brotherly affection [and] outdo one another in showing honour" (Romans 12:10)—something we will explore more deeply in the next chapter.

FOR REFLECTION

- What kind of a church results when honour is directed towards ourselves?

- How would you describe the relationship between honour and humility?

- What is the difference between vertical confession of sin and horizontal confession of sin? Why are both vital for healthy discipleship to Jesus?

- How does a gospel culture where Jesus is central and humility is normal create an environment that suffocates both self-righteousness and self-condemnation?

3. A CHURCH THAT IS BIBLICALLY COMPETITIVE

Some of us grew up way too competitive.

And by "us", I mainly mean "me".

I grew up way too competitive. During my primary school years, it didn't matter what it was. Basketball on the driveway. Football in the park. Getting to the front seat of the car. Scrabble. In-class exams. Eating dinner. Even math—perhaps you remember the "Around-the-World" math game of speed multiplication questions? During my 3rd grade to 5th grade years in school I went undefeated, and can vividly recall to this day the collective groan of the rest of my class whenever it was my turn to play. Because whatever it was, with whomever was involved, I fully intended to finish fast and finish first. I wanted to win.

That kind of competitiveness may have made me a decent athlete or student, pushing me to excel, but it also made me a terrible friend and family member. I was never really able to celebrate the successes of those around me, because I wrongly saw success as a zero-sum game. In my mind, if others won, I didn't. The more that others had, the less I had.

That kind of competitiveness—so often admired in sports or some sectors of the business world—is utterly destructive within the church. In fact, the apostle Paul warns specifically against this kind of measuring of ourselves against one another in Galatians 5:15, writing, "But if you bite and devour one another, watch out that you are not consumed by one another". A few sentences later, in verses 19-21, he warns that those who practise these "works of the flesh ... will not inherit the kingdom of God". It's a list that opens and closes with some of the more obvious sins like "sexual immorality ... idolatry ... drunkenness, orgies, and things like these". But right there in the middle is an important sequence of less obvious yet similarly destructive works, each of which has to do with a failure to rightly honour one another. Without minimising the seriousness of the other sins listed, read Paul's train of thought with just the relational words listed, to get a sense of the gravity with which God views them:

> Now the works of the flesh are evident ... enmity, strife, jealousy, fits of anger, rivalries, dissensions, divisions, envy ... I warn you, as I warned you before, that those who do such things will not inherit the kingdom of God.

Evidently, the way that we who profess Christ treat one another is a really big deal. As Francis Schaeffer pointed out in "Two Contents, Two Realities", his 1974 address to the first Lausanne Congress on World Evangelism, there are four things absolutely vital to a flourishing Christianity in our present day. The two contents are (1) sound doctrine, and (2) honest answers to honest questions, both of which we have explored in chapters 1 and 2. The two realities are (3) true spirituality and (4) the beauty of human relationships. By "true spirituality", Schaeffer means there must be "something real of the work of Christ in [our] moment-by-moment life ... through the indwelling of the Holy Spirit".[7] And without "the beauty of human relationships" our spiritual lives lack authenticity. As Schaeffer goes on to say, "If we do not show beauty in the way we treat each other, then in the eyes of the world and in the eyes of our own children, we are destroying the truth we proclaim".[8] A striving, posturing, glory-hungry competitiveness has no place within any church that claims to have a high view of God's word. No matter how sound our theology or how solid our teaching, a church that is absent of a genuine spiritual family connection has no legitimate claim to practicing orthodox Christianity.

There is, however, one exception where Christians are called to compete with one another. Of every command

---

7 Francis Schaeffer, *The Complete Works of Francis Schaeffer: Volume 3* (Crossway, 1982), p 417.

8 Schaeffer, *The Complete Works of Francis Schaeffer: Volume 3*, p 419.

given to God's people in the Bible, there is one biblical instruction in which followers of Jesus are encouraged to enter into with a robust, Spirit-powered competitiveness: *honouring one another.*

OUTDO ONE ANOTHER IN SHOWING HONOUR

It is entirely possible that Romans 12:10 is the most under-practised and frequently-minimised biblical command in the 21st-century church. Read it carefully and slowly:

> *Love one another with brotherly affection. Outdo one another in showing honour.*

According to Paul, love and honour belong together; both have a quality of selflessness to them that rejoices over other people. Christians are not merely to tolerate one another but to love one another like family. Christians are not merely to "think well of one another" or "be nice to one another" or even simply "honour one another". Christians are called to *outdo one another* in showing honour—or as the CSB puts it, "take the lead in honouring one another". Here we see initiative and intentionality. A radically reoriented posture, in light of the gospel, in which we choose to hold nothing positive back from each other in both word and action.

This may be unfamiliar ground for many of us. For example, and as I have previously mentioned, I am Australian. This means I am bilingual, possessing the ability to speak both English and Sarcasm. Fluently. It is not uncommon for those who aren't familiar with Australian culture to hear two Australians verbally poking one another and to mistake good-natured playfulness for outright hostility. And while friendly banter is certainly fine and there are times that even Jesus seemed to use hyperbolic mockery (camels through needles, anyone?), those of us with quick wits and quicker tongues would do well to remember that the word "sarcasm" finds its origins in a Greek word that literally means, "to tear the flesh off"—which has an eerily similar sounding ring to Paul's warning about biting and devouring one another in Galatians 5.

More important than my earthly citizenship (and yours) is our heavenly citizenship. And as citizens of the world to come, our words are to be spoken to one another with an unmistakably Christian accent. Our actions and generosity towards one another are to carry an undeniable aroma of Christ. And should we fear coming across as fake or insincere or in danger of "puffing people up" a little too much, we need only remember that if we are going to err, the competition woven into this biblical command ought to compel us to err on the side of a bit too much honour, love, praise, thoughtfulness, generosity and encouragement—rather than not enough. After all, there is not a single person in your church or in mine who is feeling over-encouraged right now. You have never met that person. But in a church environment of biblical competitiveness—nobody loses. Nobody is diminished. Nobody becomes poorer. Everyone becomes wealthier with the riches of relational beauty, which will outlast all the treasures of this world.

And should we need any more convincing, next time you gather with your brothers and sisters in Christ, look into their eyes and remember that you are looking at a living, breathing miracle. You are staring at someone of whom Paul would declare possesses "the glorious wealth of this mystery, which is Christ in you, the hope of glory" (Colossians 1:27 CSB). Honour and glory belong together. In light of that, why should you hold back when you consider that "your church is a holy, sacred, blood-bought *glory* in the making"?[9]

Not too long ago, I was at a leaders' retreat for Acts 29—a global, cross-denominational, church planting network—with around 50 or so staff members from different parts of the world. After praying, planning and collaborating together for a couple of days, our final session was dedicated exclusively to practising Romans 12:10. Each person in the room was, in their own time, to stand up and say something true about someone else in the room—publicly honouring them and thanking God for them. Insincerity and sarcasm were not permitted, nor was hungering to be publicly honoured. The point wasn't that everyone present *received* honour, but that everyone present had the opportunity to *practise honouring*.

---

9 Ray Ortlund and Sam Allberry, *You're Not Crazy: Gospel Sanity for Weary Churches* (Crossway, 2023), p 64.

At first, it was a little awkward. I realised that we are so used to criticism and nuancing our opinions of one another that to spend 45 minutes doing nothing but honouring and thanking God for one another felt, in some ways, like learning an entirely new world. But it was a new world that felt like *home*. This was the way the world once was before it was fractured by sin; the way the world is meant to be; the way the world will one day be again when Jesus wipes away every tear, along with every sin, once-and-for-all. To truly give ourselves to competition in the way we honour each other is to swim against the current of our present age. But that is the noble calling that is part of our gospel inheritance, that Scripture calls us to embrace with competitive energy.

COUNT OTHERS AS MORE SIGNIFICANT THAN YOURSELF

After Romans 12:10, a second important passage that is marked with biblical competitiveness is Philippians 2:3. Here Paul similarly commands us: "Do nothing from selfish ambition or conceit, but in humility count others more significant than yourselves" (ESV). He calls us to put away "selfish ambition" (which is another way of saying hungering for self-glory), and instead work together to cultivate a community that is notorious for humility. But notice how Paul describes that humility playing out in our relationships: we are to "count others more significant" than ourselves. That's what honour looks like. This perfectly captures the definition of honour in "giving weight to" one another. We are not instructed to count other Christians as more significant than ourselves only if we feel they *are* more significant than us; but to treat all *as if they are.* Even when we think they're not— *especially* when we think they're not. We would do well to remember Paul's reminder that "the parts of the body that seem to be weaker are indispensable" (1 Corinthians 12:22). As the philosopher and theologian Dallas Willard wrote:

> *If you want to experience the flow of love as never before, the next time you are in a competitive situation, pray that the others around you will be more outstanding, more praised, and more used of God than yourself. Really pull for them and rejoice for their successes. If Christians were universally to do this for each other, the earth would soon be filled with the knowledge of God's glory.*[10]

How many foolish and unnecessary divisions within the church would be resolved if we committed to treat other Christians with whom we disagree on important personal, political, and theological issues, in the spirit of Philippians 2:3? This doesn't mean losing our convictions. It means exercising them in a way where correction is brought in a biblical way that refuses to dehumanise another. As Paul says elsewhere, "The Lord's servant must not be quarrelsome but kind to everyone, able to teach, patiently enduring evil, correcting his opponents

---

10 Dallas Willard, *The Spirit of the Disciplines: Understanding How God Changes Lives,* (Harper Collins, 1988), p 174.

with gentleness" (2 Timothy 2:24-25). Christians who disagree with one another must still do so in the spirit of Christ. At the very least, this means we practise giving each other the benefit of the doubt when we disagree— that we refuse to live suspiciously towards one another or assume the worst of each other.

Consider the posture of George Whitefield towards John Wesley, a man he once considered a sort of "spiritual father". Whitefield and Wesley were both mightily used by God in various 18th-century revivals, and at one point prayed, preached and laboured in evangelism together. Eventually, however, they sharply parted ways due to their differing understandings of God's sovereignty in salvation. Neither were willing to bend to the other's theological position, and their relationship became strained. In a famous exchange, another minister expressed doubt to Whitefield as to whether John Wesley was even a genuine Christian. He asked Whitefield if he thought that they would see Wesley in heaven when they got there. "No, sir. I fear not," was Whitefield's striking reply. "For he will be so near the throne, and we shall be at such a distance, that we shall hardly get sight of him."[11] That's what it looks like to "outdo one another in showing honour" and "to count others as more significant" than yourself, even in disagreement.

---

11 J.C. Ryle, *The Christian Leaders of the Last Century* (T. Nelson and Sons, 1869), p 60.

So how might we practically do this within our churches and create a relational culture marked by a zealousness to lay down ourselves in order to build one another up? Here are two very doable and simple ways that we can put these biblical imperatives around honouring each other into practice.

ARRIVE BEFORE OTHERS

This may seem small, but don't underestimate the impact of your welcoming presence. When you arrive early to church meetings, it communicates that you are there not merely as a *consumer*, but a ready and engaged contributor. Of course there are plenty of times where things unavoidably go sideways and delay your arrival. I get it. Life happens. Perhaps you overslept or lost track of time. Perhaps you attempted to get small children ready, only for one of those children—mere moments before you get in the car—to inform you they've lost a shoe, or to start throwing the mother of all tantrums because their socks feel "scratchy", or to spontaneously take off all their clothes and declare they need to poop. And there you are as a family of frustrated, crying, naked people, trying to make it to church on time. Hypothetically, of course...

My point is that if we *always* walk in late or *constantly* rush out early, our actions declare, "I'm here primarily for myself". It may require some reshaping of your Sunday habits, but one way you could "in humility count others more significant than yourselves" (Philippians 2:3) is by arriving a little earlier than others might, in order to welcome and serve them. Think of it like this: if you invite some guests over to dinner at your home at 6 p.m., that's the time *they* are to arrive. Not you. When it's your house, there is a greater responsibility to serve and honour those who have been invited in. If your church service starts at 9 a.m., that's the time for visitors and new people to arrive. Not us. What would it look like for you to leave your home even ten minutes earlier and leave your worship service ten minutes later, simply to create some space where you might intentionally seek out, encourage, bless, or be present with someone else?

GATHER THOUGHTFULLY

A second simple yet practical way to cultivate relationships of honour within your church is not just that you *turn up* to church, but *how* you turn up. In Hebrews 10:24-25 we are reminded, "And let us consider how to stir up one another to love and good works, not neglecting to meet together, as is the habit of some, but encouraging one another, and all the more as you see the Day drawing near". Take a moment to consider the word "consider". It means "to think carefully about; to look attentively to". God wants his people, when they come together, to do so not just habitually but *thoughtfully*. And what he desires we give attention and thoughtfulness to, is considering *how* we might "stir up one another to love and good works" (v 25). The CSB uses even stronger language, calling us to "provoke" one another to love and good works! That's competitive language. As all of us who have a younger sibling or two knows, the point of provocation is to get a desired reaction. In our case, as followers of Jesus, it is a reaction of "love and good works". So, when you arrive at church or your small group this week (a bit earlier than usual, obviously), come considerately—not as a consumer within an audience, but as a member of God's family. Turn up with a willingness and thoughtfulness that wonders, "Who can I welcome today with the love of Christ? How can I be biblically provocative today with love and good works? Who does God want me to encourage and pray for before I go home?"

When we refuse to give in to an insider mentality, consumer tendency, and self-preoccupied standoffishness, and begin turning up with a Matthew 10:8 intentionality that declares *freely I have received, so freely will I give*, our churches will become outposts of relational beauty that point to the world to come. And here, in the place of authentic, sincere, omnidirectional honour, we will know something of the Lord's Prayer—"your kingdom come ... on earth as it is in heaven" (Matthew 6:10)—as a present reality in our normal rhythms of discipleship. Imagine your church as a prayerful, proactive people who see the glory of God in one another and seek to outdo one another in showing thoughtful encouragement and life-giving honour; stirring each other up to greater heights of Christlike love. Who wouldn't want to be part of a church like that?

FOR REFLECTION

- Think about the difference between unhealthy competitiveness among Christians and healthy competitiveness. What are the main differences? How can you cultivate the latter this week?

- Along with arriving a little earlier and gathering thoughtfully, can you think of any other practical ways that you can apply the commands of Romans 12:10 and Philippians 2:3 towards others in your church?

- Take a moment to pray for your church. As the Holy Spirit brings a person or two to mind, why don't you send them a text that sincerely honours them and thanks God for them.

4. A CHURCH WITH AN HONOURABLE WITNESS

Have you ever experienced opposition from someone—not because you were being rude or a jerk but because of Christ in you and your devotion to him? For those of us living in the post-Christian West, it doesn't require a PhD in sociology to see that Christianity isn't exactly culturally *hot* right now. In his excellent book *Being the Bad Guys*, Stephen McAlpine points out that Christians were once seen as the good guys, "the solution to what was the bad". But then something shifted in the eyes of the surrounding culture. McAlpine goes on to write:

Over the course of the twentieth century we became just one of the guys: one option among many ... If Christianity worked for you, fine; if it doesn't work for me, also fine. Most of us think we still live in that world ... But the problem is that that's not where we are now. The tide has shifted further. Increasingly Christianity is viewed as the bad guy. Christianity is no longer an option; it's a problem.[12]

Many of us are learning in new ways what it means to be opposed, slandered and misunderstood by our neighbours and co-workers. The post-Christian context of the West is different to pre-Christian Rome in a number of ways, but we are experiencing some similarities to what our brothers and sisters in Christ faced in the early days of the church. And there is much to learn from them, especially when it comes to living as an honourable people within an increasingly hostile world.

LESSONS FROM THE EARLY CHURCH

In the early 2nd century, just a few decades after John—the last of the apostles—passed away, a letter was written by an unnamed author to a Roman named Diognetus. The point of the letter, commonly known today as *The Epistle to Diognetus*, was to give an explanation of Christianity and why it was spreading so rapidly across the Roman Empire. And much of the letter outlined the otherworldly beauty with which Christians treated not only one another but outsiders. The impact was that in a Roman world, where human life was not held in high esteem and human dignity was conferred only upon the powerful, Christianity *humanised* people. The writer explained to Diognetus:

---

12 Stephen McAlpine, *Being the Bad Guys: How to Live for Jesus in a World that Says You Shouldn't* (The Good Book Company, 2021), p 10.

*[Christians] dwell in their own countries, but simply
as sojourners. As citizens, they share in all things with
others and yet endure all things as if foreigners. Every
foreign land is to them as their native country, and
every land of their birth as a land of strangers. They
marry, as do all [others]; they beget children; but they
do not destroy their offspring. They have a common
table, but not a common bed. They are in the flesh, but
they do not live after the flesh. They pass their days
on earth but they are citizens of heaven. They obey the
prescribed laws, and at the same time surpass the laws
by their lives. They love all men, and are persecuted
by all. They are unknown and condemned; they are
put to death, and restored to life. They are poor, yet
make many rich; they are in lack of all things, and yet
abound in all;* **they are dishonoured, and yet in their
very dishonour are glorified. They are evil spoken
of, and yet are justified; they are reviled, and
bless; they are insulted, and repay the insult with
honour.**[13]

These early Christians honoured the marriage bed; they
honoured the lives of infants and children by treating
them with compassionate love instead of discarding them
as an inconvenience; they honoured the authorities over
them, surpassing the laws of the land by the love with
which they lived; and even when they were dishonoured

---

13 "The Epistle to Diognetus", trans. Joseph Barber Lightfoot and J. R. Harmer, *The
Apostolic Fathers* (Macmillan and Co., 1891), p 506.

by all, they were glorified in their dishonour by blessing when reviled and repaying insults with honour.

We have seen from Romans 12:10 what honour looks like towards other Christians. But just a few verses later, Paul shows how that posture of honour is to mark our interactions with outsiders:

> *Bless those who persecute you; bless and do not curse ...*
> *Do not repay anyone evil for evil. Give careful thought*
> *to do what is honourable in everyone's eyes. If possible,*
> *as far as it depends on you, live at peace with everyone.*
> (Romans 12:14, 17-18, CSB)

Honour is intrinsic to the ethic of Christian living. In a world of anger and dishonour, Paul is saying that followers of Jesus are to face hostility the way that Jesus did—to endure hardship and opposition *honourably*. This is what it looks like to "not be conformed to this world" (v 2). Paul goes as far as to say that when experiencing persecution and evil at the world's hands, we should "give thought to do what is honourable in the sight of all" (v 17). What an incredible thought! And what an impossible request, apart from the empowering presence of the Holy Spirit in our lives. As far as it was within their power, believers were to cultivate peacefulness with those who were hostile towards them. They were to bless them, to seek their good, to love their enemies—for that is exactly how they were loved by Christ when they were once his enemies.

How different a posture this is to that of some believers in our own time, when facing opposition from the world. One of the common—yet wrong—responses to cultural hostility is a fundamentalist tendency (generally driven by anger or fear) that tends to view unbelievers primarily as opponents to be defeated rather than as neighbours to be loved. An "us versus them" mentality about those who hate us often forgets that these men and women are image bearers of God, who need to both hear the good news as well as see its redemptive, transforming power at work in our own lives. Honour, as it turns out, is a vital part of God's strategy for his glory being made known in the world.

HONOUR AS A MISSIONAL VIRTUE

The Christian ethic of honour is not only a biblical command; it is a missional virtue. Honour humanises those around us, along with those who oppose us. It adorns our message with an undeniable attractiveness that cannot be found anywhere else on earth. The post-apostolic church in the time of Diognetus continued to practise what Paul both commanded in word and commended by his own life. We see similar teaching from the apostle Peter as well. Writing during the time of Nero—one of the most brutal and corrupt dictators to ever govern a people—Peter says to the Christians of his day:

Beloved, I urge you as sojourners and exiles to abstain from the passions of the flesh, which wage war against

> *your soul. Keep your conduct among the Gentiles*
> *honourable, so that when they speak against you as*
> *evildoers, they may see your good deeds and glorify God*
> *on the day of visitation ... Honour everyone. Love the*
> *brotherhood. Fear God. Honour the emperor.*
>
> *(1 Peter 2:11-12, 17)*

Peter reminds Christians that to belong to Jesus is to be known as "sojourners and exiles" in this world. In the Old Testament, God's people were sometimes exiled because of their disobedience. In the New Testament, however, God's people are exiles because of their obedience. We shouldn't be surprised when faithfulness to Jesus leads to hatred from the world. Jesus explicitly promised it to his followers in John 15:19: "If you were of the world, the world would love you as its own; but because you are not of the world, but I chose you out of the world, therefore the world hates you". Christians should be the last people to go looking for trouble, but we also shouldn't be shocked when it turns up on our doorstep. Peter says as much later in his letter, reminding Christians in his own time to "not be surprised at the fiery trial when it comes upon you to test you, as though something strange were happening to you ... If you are insulted for the name of Christ, you are blessed, because the Spirit of glory and of God rests upon you" (1 Peter 4:12, 14).

Pause for a moment and take note again of who is writing these words. *Peter!* This frequently impulsive, "ready-shoot-aim" disciple has come a long way since the early years of his apprenticeship to Jesus. In the Garden of Gethsemane, when soldiers laid hands on Jesus to arrest him, Peter had pulled out a sword and sliced a guy's ear off. (Just for the record, no one in the heat of a fight actually *tries* to cut off an ear. Peter was surely aiming for his head—and missed.) Now, about three decades later, Peter has learned what it means to truly follow Jesus when being persecuted by the world. Instead of responding in indignation with force, he calls his readers to counter opposition by continuing to do good, to be unsurprised by troubles, to count the world's hatred a blessing and press on in faithful witness. When believers conduct themselves honourably, their lives become living proof of the power of the gospel that silences slander and endorses the Christian message. If we are hated by the world, it should be *because* we look like Jesus, not because we have masked our own self-serving tendencies with spiritual language.

This is Peter's great concern for the church: that followers of Jesus would embrace their calling and unmistakably reflect their Redeemer in the face of suffering. "For to this you have been called, because Christ also suffered for you, *leaving you an example*, so that you might follow in his steps" (1 Peter 2:21, emphasis added). In a world of angry voices demanding we pick a side, here is the way to preserve both our sanity and our witness: *we remember that Jesus has given us an example to follow.* So we should not be surprised by opposition from the world. Nor should we be afraid. The Lord Jesus walked willingly towards a cross, "entrusting himself to him who judges justly" (v 23). And at the cross, Jesus gives us not only the most unexpected of gifts; he leaves us with the most unexpected example of how to live and how to die when opposition comes our way.

CONVICTION WITH GENTLENESS

Another way that honour commends the gospel to outsiders is not only in the way believers live, but in the way they speak about their hope in Christ. Paul reminds us in Colossians 4:5 to "act wisely toward outsiders, making the most of the time" (CSB). And one way we are to do so, he goes on to point out, is with our words. "Let your speech always be gracious, seasoned with salt, so that you may know how you should answer each person" (v 6, CSB). Christians are to not only look different, but *sound* different. Again, Peter says something similar regarding the words of believers when unbelievers question, slander, or speak evil about them:

> But even if you should suffer for righteousness' sake, you will be blessed. Have no fear of them, nor be troubled, but in your hearts honour Christ the Lord as holy, always being prepared to make a defence to anyone who asks you for a reason for the hope that is in you; yet do it with gentleness and respect, having a good conscience, so that, when you are slandered, those who revile your good behaviour in Christ may be put to shame. (1 Peter 3:14-16)

We don't need to be afraid or troubled by the world's hatred when we are hated for the sake of Christ. "In your hearts honour Christ the Lord as holy," Peter reminds us. To be holy means to be "set apart, to be unlike anything else". That's who Jesus is—and Peter is saying, *Remember that Jesus is worth it! Whatever comes your way, Jesus is worth it! Honour Christ the Lord as holy at the very centre of your being.* When we do honour him in that way, we experience (1) a conviction that we both live out and readily defend, and (2) a gentleness towards those who don't yet share that conviction. Both deeply matter. Biblical conviction without gentleness is hypocrisy. And gentleness without clear gospel conviction is spiritual impotence. Both dishonour Christ. How are Christians to respond when they are slandered by the world? By holding fast to the gospel—to Jesus as the reason for our hope—and by doing so with "gentleness and respect ... so that, when you are slandered, those who revile your good behaviour in Christ may be put to shame" (v 15-16).

So, our understanding of faithfulness to God's mission needs to go deeper than just "Did I say the *truth* of the gospel?" We must also ask ourselves, "Am I revealing the beauty of the gospel in the *way* that I share gospel truths?" When unbelievers lash out at us, we don't reciprocate in kind or clap back. We remember that "calm is our prophetic edge"[14], and continue to honour Christ in our works and our words. A great danger to us in our times of

---

14 Ray Ortlund, in a tweet dated December 14, 2020 that is no longer available.

perpetual outrage is the temptation to "defend the faith" by using the same weapons as our opponents. While I am no fan of the 19th-century nihilist philosopher Friedrich Nietzsche, I can wholeheartedly commend his warning in this regard: "Beware that, when fighting monsters, you yourself do not become a monster ... For when you gaze long into the abyss, the abyss gazes also into you."[15]

What kind of reputation will Christians have in our time? When the world looks at our social-media feeds, will they see dignity in the way we speak of those we disagree with? Or will we reinforce their pre-existing assumptions that Christians are the judgmental folks who only care about themselves? When we are belittled, we must learn to bless. When we are reviled, we must respond respectfully. A non-negotiable part of our calling involves treating those around us with dignity by our honourable lives.

HUMANISING YOUR WORLD WITH HONOUR

In May 2023, Dr Tim Keller—a giant of the Christian faith for this present generation—passed away after a three-year battle with pancreatic cancer. I can think of no one who has embodied 1 Peter 3:15-16 more. There was no doubt that Tim was intellectually brilliant, possessing an ability to speak biblical truth into complex real-world situations like few others could. But what made Tim compelling was not just *what* he said, but *how*

---

15 Friedrich Nietzsche, *Beyond Good and Evil* (Cambridge University Press, 2002), p 69.

he would say it. His witness was more than just true. It was kind. Christlike. Overflowing with "gentleness and respect" towards both sceptics and critics alike, yet never wavering from the primacy and centrality of the gospel. I believe that what helped him embody the tension of conviction with gentleness was that his theology didn't start in Genesis 3 with humanity's sinfulness, but in Genesis 1 with humanity's dignity. Both are vital, but when we begin in Genesis 3, we tend to see people as *sinners who are hostile to God and in need of saving*, which is true but incomplete. People are, first and foremost, made in the image of God. Here is how Keller articulated this doctrine of the *imago Dei* in one of his sermons:

> *This is what this means: every person who comes across your path you need to treat with a sacredness, a reverence, a respect, a concern for their individuality, a kindness; never writing people off … It's a radical doctrine. We must treat everyone with grace, everyone with gentleness, everyone with respect—with reverence. Do you?*[16]

And in that way, Keller humanised those who disagreed with him, representing their views in the most charitable way, while presenting the gospel with conviction and beauty. A robust understanding of the *imago Dei* is the foundation of our honour towards one another, for by it we each bear the stamp of God's authority. Even our

---

16 Timothy J. Keller, "In the Image of God", https://gospelinlife.com/downloads/in-the-image-of-god-5980/ (accessed May 20, 2023).

opponents were created by him and reflect something of his likeness. It is on those grounds that the apostle Peter could say, "Honour everyone ... Honour the emperor" (1 Peter 2:17)—the latter being Nero, whose persecution of the church in the coming years would eventually result in Peter's own execution. Yet in this way, Christians turned the Roman world upside down. And when we go the same way, embracing that tension, the church of our time will become a haven of honour. A community of the cross that invites those who have known only the dehumanising existence of life under their own rule, to come and be dignified in a way that only the gospel can.

FOR REFLECTION

- What do you notice about the reputation of the early church that you'd like to see more of in your own life? How about in your own church?

- How is the presence of honour in our lives part of God's missional strategy for reaching the world with the gospel?

- Read 1 Peter 3:15 again. What happens to our witness as Christians if we are missing either gospel convictions or gentleness of spirit?

- How does a deeper commitment to the doctrine of the imago Dei change the way we interact with people we don't like or who don't like us?

5. A CHURCH LED BY HONOURABLE LEADERS

So far, we've looked primarily at honouring God and honouring one another. Honour is a posture that recognises glory, in turn leading us to "give weight" to the one being honoured; whether that's God (on account of his glory), one another (on account of God's glory being imprinted on each person through their *imago Dei*), or to those in positions of authority (on account that such authority—and all authority for that matter, according to Romans 13:1—comes from God). It is to the last aspect—honouring church leaders—that we now turn our attention. This means that, in these final chapters, I am writing not only about my fellow Christian leaders but to them.

But before we look at the biblical imperative of *honouring* leaders within the church, we need to clear a few things up. The kind of leaders that we are called to esteem, give weight to, and honour *within* the body of Christ are *honourable* leaders. The writers of the New Testament honour *faithful* leaders and call God's people to do likewise. They do not honour unfaithful leaders. On the contrary, they warn believers to have nothing to do with them. At the end of his letter to the church in Rome, Paul concludes:

> *I urge you, brothers and sisters, to watch out for those who cause divisions and put obstacles in your way that are contrary to the teaching you have learned. Keep away from them. For such people are not serving our Lord Christ, but their own appetites. By smooth talk and flattery they deceive the minds of naïve people.*
>
> (Romans 16:17-18, NIV)

Jude likewise warns against false teachers, "who cause divisions, worldly people, devoid of the Spirit" (Jude 19) as does Peter, who reminds the church of his day that "false prophets also arose among the people, just as there will be false teachers among you ... And in their greed they will exploit you with false words" (2 Peter 2:1, 3). We are not called to honour—give weight to—leaders like this.

TOUCH NOT THE LORD'S ANOINTED?

Perhaps, however, you have heard someone reference the Old Testament teaching of 1 Samuel 24:6 or Psalm 105:15, that warns *Touch not the Lord's anointed*. These words have sometimes been used in ways that are spiritually manipulative to excuse the sin of leaders or avoid questions asked in good faith. I'm talking here about any leadership ethic or culture that, out of a misguided sense of "honour", elevates a leader to a place where they are beyond any kind of critique or genuine challenge. And while we most certainly *are* to honour faithful leaders within the church, there are two primary reasons why Christian leaders have no legitimate claim to this idea.

First, the expression of "the Lord's anointed" speaks to the way in which the kings of Israel were divinely designated by God to rule that nation, being anointed with oil by a prophet (1 Samuel 10:1; 16:13). While there may be some similarities between the authority of church leaders in the New Testament and the kings or political leaders of Israel in the Old Testament, the two are not even close to being synonymous. The political authority of rulers is not the same as the spiritual authority of elders. Far from it. If anything, pastors and elders in the New Testament church have more in common with the spiritual leadership of "priests" in the Old Testament, who prayed over the people, cared for their spiritual needs, and were the primary teachers of the Scriptures. To my fellow pastors: in the now YouTube-infamous words of my friend Matt Chandler, "You're not David!"

Second, these reference verses do not prohibit critiquing or correcting a leader but *killing* them (1 Samuel 24:6; 2 Samuel 1:14). That's what David refused to do to Saul, as he tells him in 1 Samuel 24:10. Yet David himself, once he was reigning as king, was soundly and publicly rebuked by the prophet Nathan for his sins (2 Samuel 12:1-14). And David did not respond with "touch not the Lord's anointed", but with repentance. In the New Testament, Paul was not afraid to publicly confront Peter when the latter was acting hypocritically (Galatians 2:11-14), and, in fact, tells Timothy, "Do not admit a charge against an elder except on the evidence of two or three witnesses. [But] as for those who persist in sin, rebuke them in the presence of all, so that the rest may stand in fear" (1 Timothy 5:19-20).

There are, unfortunately, dishonourable leaders within the church. And we are not called to honour them, far less to obey them.

But at the same time, the presence of such leaders and their harmful misuse of authority should not cause us to abandon the biblical instruction to honour our leaders. Rather, we should have our eyes open to the kind of leaders that Scripture *does* call us to honour— *honourable* leaders—which is what the vast majority of leaders within the church, by the grace of God, seek to be. Here are five ways that Scripture describes the faithfulness of such leaders within the church: they possess Christlikeness of character, they teach God's word, they pray for the church, they care for the church, and they lead the church.

HONOURABLE LEADERS ARE FAITHFULLY CHRISTLIKE

When the New Testament lists the qualifications for church leaders in 1 Timothy 3 and Titus 1, those lists are concerned primarily with one thing: character. The late Howard Hendricks famously said that "the greatest crisis in the world today is a crisis of leadership, and the greatest crisis in leadership is a crisis of character".[17] Paul reminds Timothy in 1 Timothy 4 to, "set the believers an example in speech, in conduct, in love, in faith, in purity" (v 12) and to "pay close attention to your life and your teaching; persevere in these things, for in doing this you will save both yourself and your hearers" (v 16, CSB). Theological faithfulness and personal faithfulness are equally important in God's eyes for leaders within the church. If either is missing, leaders will, as the 17th-century pastor and commentator Matthew Henry put it, "pull down with one hand what they build up with the other".[18] Honourable leaders are biblically qualified leaders; and biblically-qualified leaders are Christlike leaders.

Paul writes, in 1 Timothy 3:1, that any man who aspires to the office of elder or overseer in a local church "desires a noble work" (CSB) or an "honourable position" (NLT). Therefore, the elders of a church are to be "above

---

17 Aubrey Malphurs, *Being Leaders: The Nature of Authentic Leadership* (Baker Publishing Group, 2003), p 18.

18 Matthew Henry, *Matthew Henry's Commentary: Volume 5, Matthew to John* (Hendrickson Publishers, 2009), p 46.

reproach" (1 Timothy 3:2, Titus 1:6), which means they have no patterns of conspicuous immorality. It includes faithfulness in marriage (1 Timothy 3:2), faithfulness in conduct (v 2-3), and faithfulness in the home (v 4-5). Such character isn't formed overnight; it comes with time and testing, which is why elders should not be new converts (v 6). They are to be marked by an unmistakable maturity and faithfulness in every area of their lives, including their reputation with outsiders (v 7). That doesn't mean these leaders are perfect, but that they are examples of Christlikeness, worthy of imitation by their church members (see 1 Corinthians 11:1). Such leaders are worthy not only of being followed but being honoured by those under their care.

HONOURABLE LEADERS FAITHFULLY TEACH GOD'S WORD

While Christlike character is paramount, there is one vital skill required of pastors and elders: they must be "able to teach", "holding to the faithful message as taught, so that [they] will be able both to encourage with sound teaching and to refute those who contradict it (1 Timothy 3:2; Titus 1:9, CSB). Notice that there is a proactive and reactive aspect to faithful Bible-teaching. Honourable leaders must proactively encourage and build up the church with sound teaching. They shepherd by leading the flock into the green pastures of God's word again and again and again. But they must also protect their people from false teaching, refuting "those who contradict" God's word.

This is no easy task. And for that reason, James reminds us that "not many of you should become teachers, my brothers, for you know that we who teach will be judged with greater strictness" (James 3:1). On the positive side, Paul says that "the elders who rule well [should] be considered worthy of double honour, especially those who labour in preaching and teaching" (1 Timothy 5:17). In fact, look how highly Paul esteems the faithful teaching of God's word throughout his second letter to Timothy:

Do your best to present yourself to God as one approved, a worker who has no need to be ashamed, rightly handling the word of truth. (2 Timothy 2:15)

But as for you, continue in what you have learned and have firmly believed, knowing from whom you learned it and how from childhood you have been acquainted with the sacred writings, which are able to make you wise for salvation through faith in Christ Jesus. All Scripture is breathed out by God and profitable for teaching, for reproof, for correction, and for training in righteousness. (3:14-16)

I charge you in the presence of God and of Christ Jesus, who is to judge the living and the dead, and by his appearing and his kingdom: preach the word; be ready in season and out of season; reprove, rebuke, and exhort, with complete patience and teaching. (4:1-2)

Why is this so important? Because Paul knew that a time would come "when people will not endure sound teaching, but having itching ears they will accumulate for themselves teachers to suit their own passions, and will turn away from listening to the truth and wander off into myths" (2 Timothy 4:3-4). Honourable leaders do not twist Scripture to reinforce their own opinions, nor do they abandon Scripture to give a motivational talk of self-help principles. They understand it is a holy thing to speak on behalf of God. Therefore, honourable leaders do not edit God's word but faithfully deliver it.

HONOURABLE LEADERS FAITHFULLY PRAY FOR THE CHURCH

As the church grew in the aftermath of Pentecost, so too did tensions within the church. One of those is detailed in Acts 6, where the Hellenist widows were being neglected in the daily distribution of food. But rather than doing this themselves, the apostles gathered all the believers together and called them to pick out seven men of good reputation, full of the Spirit and of wisdom, who would be appointed to the ministry of serving tables and ensuring no one was overlooked (v 2-3). Their reasoning? "It is not right that we should give up preaching the word of God to serve tables ... we will devote ourselves to prayer and to the ministry of the word" (v 2, 4). In addition to faithful teaching, they understood that their highest responsibility as leaders was to pray.

Here's what sobers me: no matter how gifted I am as a leader, no matter how eloquently I preach or how successful my ministry is or how many churches I plant, the truest measure to the authenticity of my spirituality is the measure of my prayer-life. For what is prayerlessness in a pastor, but the pride of self-reliance? Charles Spurgeon gravely warns those of us who lead about neglecting this important work:

> *Ah, teachers, your closet shall be turned into the open air one day, and the contents of your secret chambers be published before the sun. Oh, you whose cobwebbed closets witness against you; oh, you against whom the beam out of the wall explaineth because your voice has not been heard there, against whom the very floor might bear witness, because it has never felt the weight of your knees...*[19]

Honourable leaders pray for their church. They know that that is the greatest need for themselves and their churches. Prayer is what connects our never-ending needs to God's never-ending grace. Prayer is the vehicle through which God has sovereignly determined to strengthen his people and accomplish his purposes in this world. Like a lamp disconnected from the wall, any church leader or church that is absent of prayer, will find themselves absent of God's power. It matters little how large the bulb is or how elegant its design or how high it sits; it cannot accomplish its purpose without power. Faithful leaders know that apart from Jesus they can do nothing (John 15:5), which is why faithful leaders are praying leaders.

---

19 Charles Spurgeon, *The New Park Street Pulpit, volume 4* (Baker Books, 1994), p 221.

HONOURABLE LEADERS FAITHFULLY CARE FOR THE CHURCH

In 1 Peter 5:1-2, we find another essential passage that outlines the leadership qualifications for those entrusted with authority within a local church:

> So I exhort the elders among you, as a fellow elder and a witness of the sufferings of Christ, as well as a partaker in the glory that is going to be revealed: shepherd the flock of God that is among you.

Take note of those last four words—often overlooked—that clarify the kind of caring leadership that Jesus the chief Shepherd requires of his under-shepherds: "Shepherd the flock of God *that is among you*" (v 2). Honourable leaders are not tyrants who domineer *over* the church; nor are they merely ministerial butlers *under* the church, ready to jump at every person's beck and call; nor are they to become specialists *outside* of the church, who exercise authority but are disconnected in their own ivory tower of leadership. Honourable leaders are *present*. They are *among* the flock. They care for the church in proximity to the church. They love the church. In the same way Christ gave himself for the church with sacrificial love, so too will those whom he has genuinely called to this work. Paul's charge to the elders of the church in Ephesus is a charge to the elders of every local church: "Pay careful attention to yourselves and to all the flock, of which the Holy Spirit has made you overseers, to care for the church of God, which he obtained with his own blood" (Acts 20:28).

This will, of course, look different in a church of 50-100 people than it will in a church of 500 people or thousands of people. It is impossible for the pastor of a church of a thousand people to personally care for each one. This is one reason why a team of elders and other qualified leaders are required for a church to flourish; to avoid unintentionally creating a culture where care for the congregation is only seen as meaningful if it comes from one particular leader. And that's unhealthy. The pastor and author Christopher Ash points out:

> If your church is large, it may be unrealistic to expect your pastor to know each individual well. If so, it is their responsibility to delegate to other leaders or elders, so that everyone in the church is known well, and prayed for individually, by at least one of them. Moses did something similar when he found the people of God were too numerous for him to care for by himself (Exodus 18:13-26). Delegation is evidence that our pastors do care for us, not that they don't.[20]

But no matter the size of a church, honourable leaders must work out how to continue shepherding the flock of God *that is among them*, resisting the temptation to disengage from genuine present care for the flock.

---

20 Christopher Ash, *The Book Your Pastor Wishes You Would Read* (The Good Book Company, 2019), p 29.

How can this be done?

I have been a pastor in churches that have ranged in size from 50 to 15,000, and have learned an important principle while navigating those varying church-size dynamics: just because I can't do something for *everyone*, it doesn't mean I shouldn't do it for *anyone*. Pastor, you may not be able to do *every* hospital visit, but do you do *any*? You may not be able to meet with *every* new person, but do you still make space to connect with *any* new people? You certainly cannot personally disciple *everyone*, but are you actively discipling *anyone*? It may feel like a tightrope at times, and we are often prone to overcorrection. But if we realise that we have done so, repentance as leaders means adjusting to a healthier posture of leadership that "shepherds the flock of God that is among you".

HONOURABLE LEADERS FAITHFULLY LEAD THE CHURCH

Finally, Christian leaders have been given legitimate authority that has been invested in them by Jesus to lead the church towards spiritual maturity, for the glory of God. Leaders are, in fact, one of the gifts that Jesus gives to his church, and have been entrusted with the responsibility of keeping their church "attentive to God".[21] Look again at the work that Peter calls elders to in 1 Peter 5:

---

21 Eugene H. Peterson, *Working the Angles: The Shape of Pastoral Integrity* (Eerdmans, 1987), p 2.

So I exhort the elders among you, as a fellow elder and a witness of the sufferings of Christ, as well as a partaker in the glory that is going to be revealed: shepherd the flock of God that is among you, exercising oversight, not under compulsion, but willingly, as God would have you; not for shameful gain, but eagerly; not domineering over those in your charge, but being examples to the flock. And when the chief Shepherd appears, you will receive the unfading crown of glory. Likewise, you who are younger, be subject to the elders. Clothe yourselves, all of you, with humility towards one another, for "God opposes the proud but gives grace to the humble".

(1 Peter 5:1-5)

Honourable leaders are those who use their God-given authority willingly and eagerly. Sadly, there are too many stories of Christian leaders in our time who have misused authority, causing some to query any exercise of genuine authority as abuse. Yet leaders must indeed *lead*. The leaders of your church are not called to simply help people, but to lead them onward into greater maturity and faithfulness to Jesus. They have been invested with real authority, but honourable leaders refuse to use it for the "shameful gain" of money, popularity, or a position of influence. Instead, they lead as those who know they will one day answer to Jesus, the chief Shepherd, for how they have used his delegated authority. To settle for anything less is an abdication of their calling. The Christian counsellor and thinker Richard Lovelace calls our attention to the deadly compromise that takes place when pastors refuse to exercise godly oversight in the leadership of their churches:

> An unconscious conspiracy arises between their flesh and that of their congregations. It becomes tacitly understood that the laity will give the pastor places of special honour in the exercise of their gifts, if the pastors will agree to leave their congregations pre-Christian lifestyles undisturbed and do not call for the mobilisation of lay gifts for the work of the kingdom. Pastors are thus permitted to become ministerial superstars. Their pride is fed and their insecurity is pacified even if they are run ragged, and their congregations are permitted to remain herds of sheep in which each has cheerfully turned to his own way.[22]

Faithful leadership requires more than just the right use of authority. It must also include the delegation of that authority if your church is to grow towards maturity. Faithful pastors don't do everything themselves, but instead understand that their role is to "equip the saints for the work of ministry, for building up the body of Christ, until we all attain to the unity of the faith and of the knowledge of the Son of God, to mature manhood, to the measure of the stature of the fullness of Christ" (Ephesians 4:12-13).

---

22 Richard F. Lovelace, *Dynamics of Spiritual Life: An Evangelical Theology of Renewal* (Paternoster Press, 1979), p 207.

This includes empowering other leaders—sometimes referred to as deacons or coworkers—who use their gifts to build up the church. The New Testament is filled with men and women alike who, though not elders, still carried significant leadership weight within the church. In Romans 16, Paul lists a number of other leaders whom he greets, commends and honours. One such leader is "Phoebe, a servant of the church at Cenchreae". Paul instructs the church at Rome to "welcome her in the Lord in a way worthy of the saints, and help her in whatever she may need from you, for she has been a patron of many and of myself as well" (v 1-2). Also listed are the leaders "Prisca and Aquila, my coworkers in Christ Jesus, who risked their own necks for my life. Not only do I thank them, but so do all the Gentile churches" (v 3-4, CSB). The list goes on to include 24 more names, many of whom Paul honours as "coworker[s] in Christ ... who have worked hard in the Lord" (v 9, 12 CSB). Our churches ought to be sanctuaries of honour that do likewise; esteeming honourable leaders who labour in service to God and his people. For when a church experiences faithfulness from their leaders—in their character, their teaching, their prayers, their care and their leadership—an environment is created where honour is gladly and readily given. To this final important piece, we now turn.

FOR REFLECTION

- What are some differences that come to your mind when you think about honourable versus dishonourable leaders?

- Which of those five characteristics of honourable leaders would you like to see more of in the church? Why?

- Think of an example of honourable Christian leadership that you have experienced. What stands out to you about that leader?

6. A CHURCH THAT RIGHTLY HONOURS SUCH LEADERS

Leadership of any kind is difficult. Leadership within the church is a sacred, weighty, exhausting, wonderful calling. It is sacred because it is a calling that comes directly from God. It is weighty because it involves the eternal destinies of those under their charge. It is exhausting because it is never-ending—there is always another sermon to prepare and preach, person to care for, conflict to mediate and problem to solve. It is wonderful because while it's true that leaders have a front-row seat to the most difficult moments of sin and sorrow in people's lives, they also are privileged to see the most beautiful moments of redemption, joy, growth and newness of life.

How can we honour those who labour in such important work on behalf of God and his people? What does honouring such leaders look like according to Scripture?

In one sense, this final chapter is what every pastor wishes their people would know; an inside look into the longings and prayers of Christian leaders who desire to honour Jesus and see their church do likewise. There are no perfect Christian leaders, just as there are no perfect Christian churches. So honour ought not be withheld from our leaders or from one another in our churches until they have a perfect record. As Charles Spurgeon wrote:

> You that are members of the church have not found it perfect, and I hope that you feel almost glad that you have not. If I had never joined a church till I had found one that was perfect, I should never have joined one at all; and the moment I did join it, if I had found one, I should have spoiled it, for it would not have been a perfect church after I had become a member of it. Still, imperfect as it is, it is the dearest place on earth to us. [23]

Every Christian, leader, and local church is a work in progress; they are a community of redeemed sinners who by the Spirit's power are growing in humility and holiness, learning to honour and love one another.

We're not always going to get it right. Over the last two decades of pastoral ministry, I have had my share of difficult situations and difficult people. I've made plenty of my own mistakes and had to repent where I got it wrong. I know first-hand what it means to be

---

23 Charles Spurgeon, *The Metropolitan Tabernacle Pulpit, volume 37* (The Banner of Truth Trust, 1970), p 633.

slandered, misrepresented, betrayed and ghosted by people. But I also know what it means to be honoured. I write this chapter as a pastor who is fortunate enough to experience the beauty of a gospel culture in the church I lead—Liberti Church. I love these precious people and feel loved by them; something I do not take for granted. Our church is not perfect by any measure, as is often revealed in one of the unofficial mottos heard frequently from our people: *"onward we stumble"*. But I can say with integrity that there are four practices, each robustly biblical, that I have seen our church extend to me and other leaders as we follow Jesus together. These are four approaches that Jesus calls every congregation to embrace—that he calls *you* to embrace—when it comes to faithful leaders in your own church:

- Follow them obediently

- Pray for them regularly

- Honour them appropriately

- Love them greatly

FOLLOW YOUR LEADERS OBEDIENTLY

The book of Hebrews concludes with a number of miscellaneous instructions on Christian living—ranging from hospitality to holiness, financial contentment to faithfulness through suffering. But another theme, and one that is given considerable attention, is how Christians are to regard their leaders. First, Christians are instructed, "Remember your leaders, those who spoke to you the word of God. Consider the outcome of their way of life, and imitate their faith" (Hebrews 13:7). Notice again the kind of leaders we are to remember and imitate—those who have faithfully taught us God's word and followed it themselves. Leaders who pay attention to both their life and their teaching (1 Timothy 4:16) are honourable examples worthy of emulation. Faithful guides like these are gifts from Jesus himself to the church, for the maturing of the church (Ephesians 4:11-13). One way that you greatly honour your leaders is by copying what you see in their own discipleship to Christ and demonstrating it in your own. Few things make them happier than seeing the Scriptures they have taught you turn into reality in your own life!

The author of Hebrews calls us to go even deeper than imitation, though, going on a few verses later to say, "Obey your leaders and submit to them, for they are keeping watch over your souls, as those who will have to give an account. Let them do this with joy and not with groaning, for that would be of no advantage to you" (v 17). To be sure, following our leaders obediently does not mean unquestioning or unconditional obedience. Our submission and obedience as Christians is first and foremost to Christ as Lord, so we should never follow leaders into sin or enable sinful leadership by refusing to speak up when necessary. But as our leaders follow Jesus and submit to Scripture, we are to obey and submit to them.

Here's the rub: obedience and submission are easy to do when we are being asked to do something that we *already want to do*. But that's not really submission; that's just agreement. Where this is really tested is when our leaders make a decision we don't like or won't do something that we want. The humbling truth for every one of us is that the truest indicator of our maturity in Christ is not how much Scripture we have read or how many services we have attended or how much responsibility we carry, but how we respond when we don't get our way. We honour our leaders when we submit to their authority, even if we disagree or don't fully understand.

Think about it like this. When we were children, we were often oblivious as to just how much our obedience and glad submission to authority meant to our parents. Frequently, we thought we knew better than they did and chafed at their directions. For those who are parents, think how much more you now appreciate the sacrifices that your own parents made for you. Consider how you watch over the well-being of your children, desiring their flourishing, readily laying yourself down on their behalf and using your authority as a parent to guide them towards maturity. In the same way that children greatly honour good parents—the God-ordained authority in their lives—through willing obedience to them, so too do Christians honour the leaders of their local church.

And here's why we can.

One day, your leaders will stand before Jesus and give an account of the way they shepherded his people. For any leader who actually loves God's word and takes it seriously, this reminder sobers us. In a sacred way, it even haunts us. Faithful shepherds of churches don't go home and "leave their work at work"; they have you on their minds. They watch over your soul in prayer. Joyful and willing obedience from the church creates an environment that benefits both shepherd and flock alike—"Let them do this with joy and not with groaning, for that would be of no advantage to you" (v 17). What wears good leaders down is "not hard hours of labour, but frustration with a hard-hearted flock. The greatest gift a Christian can give to a spiritual leader is a readiness to believe and to obey God's word".[24]

PRAY FOR YOUR LEADERS REGULARLY

A second way that we honour those in spiritual authority over us is by consistently holding them up in prayer. It's little wonder that after calling the church to obey and submit to their leaders as those who will one day "give an account" to God (v 17), that the author of Hebrews says in the very next verse, "Pray for us, for we are sure that we have a clear conscience, desiring to act honourably in all things" (Hebrews 13:18). When someone once asked Spurgeon the secret to the fruitfulness of his ministry, he responded, "My people pray for me". I could not agree

---

24 Richard D. Phillips, *Hebrews, Reformed Expository Commentary* (P&R Publishing, 2006), p 617–618.

more. A church that prays for their leaders is a church that takes seriously the spiritual battle that surrounds them. Your leaders, like you, must daily make war on sin that tries to creep into their lives. In a time like ours, marked by so many leadership scandals that stain the witness of the church to the watching world, have the leaders of your church ever needed your prayers more?

Honour your leaders by going to God on their behalf in prayer. Perhaps you might set a reminder in your phone to pray Hebrews 13:18 over their lives—that they would "have a clear conscience, desiring to act honourably in all things". Pray for their faithful endurance in the work of the ministry. Pray for their joy in the Lord. Pray for protection against spiritual attack directed towards them and their families. Pray that God would give them boldness in declaring his word. Pray that God would give them wisdom to navigate the difficult decisions and situations that your church must inevitably face. It is no easy thing to lead Christians through the tensions of our divided times.

And as you pray for them, let them know that you are doing so! I have several people in my church who have made a habit of regularly reaching out to me, in order to let me know they are praying for me. I can say with confidence that knowing my church prays for me is one of the most meaningful sources of fuel in my life. The church, at its best, is a church devoted to praying for one another. In multiple places throughout the New

Testament, we see the apostle Paul ask for the prayers of various churches (see Romans 15:30; Philippians 1:19; Colossians 4:3; Ephesians 6:19; 1 Thessalonians 5:25; 2 Thessalonians 3:1). If Paul—the multilingual, genius-intellect, church-planting, Scripture-writing, gospel-heralding apostle—needed prayer from the church, how much more do the leaders of our churches?! Your leaders rightfully and righteously covet your prayers. Honour them by praying for them.

HONOUR YOUR LEADERS APPROPRIATELY

In 1 Timothy 5, Paul points out two ways we can honour our leaders appropriately and biblically: the first is by appreciating them and their labours for the church; the second is by protecting them against unfounded accusations.

> *The elders who are good leaders are to be considered worthy of double honour, especially those who work hard at preaching and teaching. For the Scripture says: Do not muzzle an ox while it is treading out the grain, and, "The worker is worthy of his wages." Don't accept an accusation against an elder unless it is supported by two or three witnesses. (1 Timothy 5:17-19, CSB)*

First, we can see that good leaders are worthy of being appreciated with "double honour". This is particularly true for those elders "who work hard at preaching and teaching" (v 17) and faithfully feed the flock with the word of God. Such leaders are worthy of not only respectful appreciation but financial compensation. Paul's quotes from the Old Testament in verse 18 demonstrate that appropriately honouring faithful preaching and teaching by church leaders includes paying them well enough to do so. To be sure, there were times and contexts where Paul himself worked bi-vocationally to fund his ministry in various parts of the world (see Acts 18:1-4; 1 Thessalonians 2:9). Pastors must be willing to do likewise if their church is not yet financially self-sustaining. But Paul also reminds Christians that rightly honouring their leaders includes the biblical principle, "the worker is worthy of his wages" (1 Timothy 5:18 CSB). When a church fails to honour their leaders in this way, it not only adds a financial burden on top of all the other burdens their pastors carry in their oversight of the church, it also communicates "to that congregation and to the outside world how little they think of the ministry of the word of God."[25] If you do not yet contribute financially to the ministry and mission of your local church and the teaching that you receive, here is another reason to begin giving regularly, cheerfully and generously.

Second, we honour our leaders appropriately by protecting them from slander and accusations that are not grounded in the truth. The verses that immediately follow these reveal that disqualifying behaviour by church

---

25 David Platt, Daniel L. Akin, and Tony Merida, *Christ-Centered Exposition Commentary: Exalting Jesus in 1 & 2 Timothy and Titus* (B&H Publishing, 2013), p 88.

leaders is to be taken very seriously—unrepentant church leaders are to be publicly rebuked (v 20) and any hint of partiality or favouritism on account of being in leadership is prohibited (v 21). But Paul also acknowledges that any charge received against an elder in the church should only be accepted if it has multiple witnesses. While individual allegations of serious sin should never be ignored, they should also be handled carefully. Pastors will frequently be the targets of untrue and unfair accusations. The devil's name, "Satan", literally means "the accuser". So it should come as no surprise that he will work to undermine God's glory by levelling accusations at Christians generally, and Christian leaders specifically. A smear campaign of rumours and lies has the capacity to destroy your church. For this reason, Paul gives a process of protection with "two or three witnesses", so that false accusations will not derail the unity of your church by undermining the congregation's trust in the integrity of their leaders. Our churches should be places in which leaders are biblically appreciated with support and biblically protected from slander.

LOVE YOUR LEADERS GREATLY

Finally, you honour your leaders by loving them greatly. Your leaders in Christ, just like you, are people in need of knowing that they are loved. In what I believe is one of the most beautiful passages of relational tenderness in Scripture, Paul writes to the church in Thessalonica: "Now we ask you, brothers and sisters, to give recognition to those who labour among you and lead you in the Lord and admonish you, and to regard them very highly in love because of their work. Be at peace among yourselves" (1 Thessalonians 5:12-13, CSB). Think about what it means to "give recognition to" your leaders and to regard them "very high in love". What might that look like in your own context?

Here are three practical suggestions for esteeming your leaders highly in love.

First, love your leaders by relating to them personally rather than transactionally. Refuse to interact with them as if you are a spiritual customer approaching a distributor of spiritual goods and services and knowledge. You honour them greatly when you remember that they are not a ministerial superstar but a person who bears the image of God and possesses the limitations and needs woven into all of humanity. I can remember reading with grief the lament of one former pastor, who had spent time with a therapist reflecting on all the people who had "ghosted" him (that is, people who had left without reason or even the courtesy of a goodbye) over his 20 years of pastoral ministry. The list was almost 100 people long, and it contained many with whom he'd spoken with in their homes, whose children he'd baptised, who he had cried with in their pain and counselled through their crises. And his heart-breaking conclusion was that "most people see me as a resource to consume and not a relationship to consider".[26] Those words give language to the unspoken sorrow so many pastors feel. Love your leaders by humanising them and remembering that they are still a part of the family of God.

Second, love your leaders and hold them in high regard through the simple yet profoundly important ministry of presence.

When our children were younger, we had a chore chart on our fridge which, in our case at least, was a fantastic way of ensuring that both children and parents alike all felt a delightful sense of failure. Frankly, it never really worked. Nonetheless, we all laughed one morning when we discovered that Ezra—our middle child—had taken it upon himself to add a line for "Dad" complete with daily responsibilities including: "Shower. Shave. Show up." While comical, our 7-year-old understood just how valuable the act of simply "showing up" is. Do we? Don't underestimate the impact that your regular presence on a Sunday has, not only in building up the entire church, but in communicating to your leaders that you "regard them very highly in love because of their work" (v 13). As Dietrich Bonhoeffer articulated in his classic *Life Together*, "The physical presence of other Christians is a source of incomparable joy and strength to the believer"[27]—including your leaders.

---

26 Dan White Jr. on Twitter (February 27, 2019), https://twitter.com/danwhitejr/status/1100430419164626944?s=20.

27 Bonhoeffer, *Life Together*, p 8.

Third, love your leaders by having realistic expectations of them. The elders or deacons of your church cannot mechanically labour without ceasing but, like all of us, have to navigate the limits of time and place, bad moods, low energy, disappointment, and occasionally being "hangry". We honour our leaders by protecting their times of rest, allowing them to practise strategic withdrawal whether it be on their designated Sabbath day (usually not a Sunday!), family holidays, or extended times of sabbatical for renewal and endurance in the work of the ministry. Realistic expectations of them also means realistic expectations of their families. We can love our leaders and hold them in high regard by remembering that their spouses are not "free staff" for the church to lean on but fellow church members like everyone else, with whom we can strive to "outdo" in showing honour (Romans 12:10). Such thoughtfulness in love towards our leaders reciprocates the loving care they show to us, creating an environment of omnidirectional honour that glorifies God and blesses the church. In his short yet extremely helpful book that I highly recommend, *The Book Your Pastor Wishes You Would Read (but is too embarrassed to ask)*, Christopher Ash concludes:

> *There is no doubt in my mind that churches that show kindness will have still better pastors as a result; for it is only natural that their pastors will return to their pastoral leadership with a fresh determination to love and care for, to teach and preach to, and to pray for these who have loved them ... So let us not hesitate to*

pour out kindness upon our pastors, and their families if they have them. Such an eloquent expression of the love of Christ will very naturally strengthen in them a comparable kindness and love for us. Paradoxically, although we do not show kindness in order to gain benefits, we shall find ourselves pastored the better for it![28]

FOR REFLECTION

- Think of a faithful Christian leader or two in your own life. What is something you admire in their faith and walk with Jesus, that you want to imitate in your own? Take a moment to pray for them and thank God for them.

- Consider what you might be able to do this coming week that would "give recognition to those who labour among you and lead you in the Lord and admonish you, and to regard them very highly in love because of their work" (1 Thessalonians 5:12-13, CSB). Perhaps take a few minutes to honour them for something specific in their leadership through an email or a text message.

---

28 Ash, *The Book Your Pastor Wishes You Would Read*, p 85, 90.

CONCLUSION: THE ONE
WHOM GOD HONOURS

My hope, as you put this book down, is that you will give yourself with renewed zeal to honouring God first and foremost; to doing what you can to cultivate a gospel culture within your church that seeks to "outdo one another in showing honour" (Romans 12:10); to living honourably within your community, knowing that this is part of God's missional strategy for his church; and to honouring your leaders.

Honour to God. Honour to one another. Honour to our leaders. To "give weight" in each of these directions is both biblical and beautiful. To honour rightly is an act of loving self-renunciation. It is how our shared life together is meant to be, and how it one day will be, when the prayer Jesus taught his disciples to pray becomes a lived reality upon his return: "Your kingdom come ... on earth as it is in heaven" (Matthew 6:10).

But the most remarkable aspect of honour—an idea almost scandalous to even consider if it hadn't first been mentioned by Jesus himself—is that for those who follow him down the narrow road of humility in service to him, *God* will honour *them*. Jesus says so explicitly to his followers in John 12:24-26:

> *Truly, truly, I say to you, unless a grain of wheat falls into the earth and dies, it remains alone; but if it dies, it bears much fruit. Whoever loves his life loses it, and whoever hates his life in this world will keep it for eternal life. If anyone serves me, he must follow me; and where I am, there will my servant be also. If anyone serves me, the Father will honour him.*

Earlier in this book, we looked at Tozer's words: "What comes into our minds when we think about God is the most important thing about us". And while such a claim is largely true, vitally connecting our heart and our hands with the life of our mind, it's actually not the *most* important thing about us. C.S Lewis counters, "How God thinks of us is not only more important, but infinitely more important. Indeed, how we think of him is of no importance except in so far as it is related to how he thinks of us ... To be loved by God, not merely pitied, but delighted in as an artist delights in his work or a father in a son—it seems impossible, a weight or burden of glory which our thoughts can hardly sustain. But so it is."[29]

Have you ever considered, beloved Christian, that

---

29 C.S Lewis, *The Weight of Glory* (The Macmillan Co, 1966), p 10.

there is a day in your future where God the Father will *honour you* for following Jesus? After all, the way of humility that Jesus walked is ultimately a pathway into resurrection glory. Know this: the self-sacrifice required for you to truly honour those around you and over you will be difficult and costly at times. But it is never unseen by God. Your honour is never in vain. For on that final day, when we all stand before the Father, there will be no higher privilege in all the universe than being honoured by the one who sits on the throne. Honouring, as it turns out, is not only something God calls *us* to do but something that *he* delights to do. It's something that reflects his very heart.

So let's pray for and press on into the humility and patience that becoming an honourable, honouring people will require of us. In light of what our Lord Jesus has done for us, let's humble ourselves before God and one another, refusing self-exaltation and the destruction that inevitably follows it, so that the church of our time will radiate with the relational beauty that God intends for her to possess. Let's redeem this word that has been so often misused, reinfusing it with the fullness of its biblical meaning, convinced that when honour is rightly practiced, God is greatly glorified.

> *To the King of ages, immortal, invisible, the only God,*
> *be honour and glory for ever and ever. Amen.*
> *(1 Timothy 1:17)*

DISCUSSION GUIDE
FOR SMALL GROUPS

1. A CHURCH THAT HONOURS GOD ABOVE ALL

1. What is it about God that makes you want to honour him? You might like to share stories of times when you've been overcome in worship—what was it that so struck you about God in those moments?

2. Why is it so important to tell the truth about God?

3. Read Luke 6:46-49. How do Jesus' words help us understand why God cares about how we behave?

4. Read Matthew 15:1-7. In what way did the Pharisees and scribes seem to be honouring God? In what sense were they actually dishonouring him? What might be an equivalent to this today?

5. Where do you see devotion and reverence for God in your own church? Are there any areas for growth in this?

6. What about you personally? Can you identify one area in which you long to honour him more as a result of this chapter? Take some time to pray about this.

2. A CHURCH THAT IS NOTORIOUS FOR HUMILITY

1. What might your church look like if every time everyone walked into the building, their first thought was not "What am I going to get today?", but "Isn't it amazing that I'm even a Christian? Isn't it utterly ridiculous that God has extended grace to someone like me?" What difference would this make?

2. In what ways does the culture around us discourage humility?

3. Read Luke 14:8-11. In what ways did Jesus follow his own instructions here?

4. What are some ways in which we can apply Jesus' words to ourselves today—at home, at church, at work?

5. What do you think it looks like to honour one another in a way that doesn't lead us into pride?

6. What could your group do to foster a culture of humility over the coming weeks and months?

3. A CHURCH THAT IS BIBLICALLY COMPETITIVE

1. We're called to outdo one another in showing honour. How is this different from other forms of competitiveness?

2. Read Romans 12:10 and Philippians 2:3. What practical ways can you think of to apply these commands in your church?

3. Sometimes we are tempted to criticise or show our irritation with people rather than honouring them. What are some ways to help ourselves to see others in the way God would like us to see them?

4. What do you think it looks like to honour someone with whom you deeply disagree? What about someone who has treated you badly? Re-read pages 56-57 for help with this.

5. Re-read the sections "Arrive before Others" and "Gather Thoughtfully". What practical steps could you take to build up this kind of culture in your church?

6. Take some time as a group to practise honouring one another. In your own time, say something true about someone else in the room—publicly honouring them and thanking God for them.

4. A CHURCH WITH AN HONOURABLE WITNESS
Read 1 Peter 2:11-23

1. In what ways are we called to live honourably towards outsiders in these verses?

2. How does Jesus' example encourage and help us as we do so?

3. What sort of reputation do you think Christians have generally in our culture?

4. What are some good and bad ways of responding to opposition or nastiness (whether over our Christian convictions or other issues)? Share some real-life examples if you can think of them.

5. What does it look like to honour the gospel in our speech? Are there particular situations when this might be more difficult?

6. Identify the key situations and settings in which each of you interact with non-Christians. In what ways might God be challenging you to live more honourably there? Take some time to pray for one another.

5. A CHURCH LED BY HONOURABLE LEADERS
Read 1 Timothy 3:1-10; Titus 1:5-9; 2 Timothy 4:1-5

1. What key ideas about church leadership do all these passages have in common?

2. What attributes should be avoided in a church leader, according to these passages? Can you say why?

3. What leaders have you been particularly grateful for in your Christian walk? Which of the five hallmarks of honourable leadership listed in the chapter did they particularly display?

4. How has this chapter helped you assess your own expectations for church leaders? Do you ever expect too much? Or too little?

5. What do you think you could do to support your church leaders in each of the five hallmarks mentioned in the chapter?

6. How do you think you should be praying for your own church leaders in the light of what you've read and discussed? Pray for them now.

6. A CHURCH THAT RIGHTLY HONOURS SUCH LEADERS

1. Read Hebrews 13:7, 17-18. If leaders "keep watch over [our] souls", why is this a reason to obey and submit to them? Why is it a reason to pray for them?

2. When do you think we should not obey leaders? When do you think we should obey even though we find it difficult?

3. Read 1 Timothy 5:17-20. Imagine someone makes an accusation about your pastor to you. What do you think you ought to do?

4. What are the differences between relating to a leader personally and relating to them transactionally? (See page 101.)

5. Can you think of further ways of loving and appreciating church leaders, not listed in the chapter?

6. What is one step you can take this week or this month to honour a faithful leader in your church? And how can you make this a regular habit?

LOVE YOUR CHURCH

loveyourchurchseries.com

MORE FROM ADAM RAMSEY

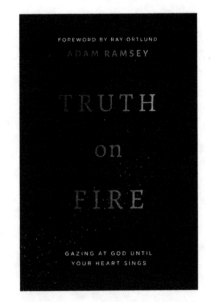

If you yearn for God but desire a clearer biblical picture of this God whom you love, or if you have been walking with God for a while now but your experience of him has become settled or dry, then this book is for you.

A BETTER WAY TO LIVE

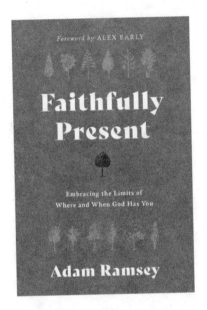

This thought-provoking book helps us to live each day faithfully present with God and with others. Discover fresh joy in the little things, freedom from the tyranny of time, and contentment in every season of life.

thegoodbook.com/present
thegoodbook.co.uk/present

the good book

COMPANY

BIBLICAL | RELEVANT | ACCESSIBLE

At The Good Book Company, we are dedicated to helping Christians and local churches grow. We believe that God's growth process always starts with hearing clearly what he has said to us through his timeless word—the Bible.

Ever since we opened our doors in 1991, we have been striving to produce Bible-based resources that bring glory to God. We have grown to become an international provider of user-friendly resources to the Christian community, with believers of all backgrounds and denominations using our books, Bible studies, devotionals, evangelistic resources, and DVD-based courses.

We want to equip ordinary Christians to live for Christ day by day, and churches to grow in their knowledge of God, their love for one another, and the effectiveness of their outreach.

Call us for a discussion of your needs or visit one of our local websites for more information on the resources and services we provide.

Your friends at The Good Book Company

thegoodbook.com | thegoodbook.co.uk
thegoodbook.com.au | thegoodbook.co.nz
thegoodbook.co.in